T0305560

The Book of My Son Reuben

"I wish I had not had to write this book because then my lovely son Reuben would still be alive," says David Cohen. "He was adorable, formidably intelligent, a loving son, a loving brother. He died far too young. He had the bad luck to have two grandparents who had addictive personalities. His efforts to resist the lure of drugs failed. And so did I."

The Book of My Son Reuben is a personal account of how psychologist David Cohen coped – and did not cope – with the death of his son, Reuben. Providing a unique perspective on the experience of parental loss, it offers a personal and analytical exploration of sorrow and guilt, and of what research tells us about trauma and grief.

Illustrated throughout with David Cohen's personal insight into how he continues to navigate his loss, this honest book provides a deeper understanding of loss for parents who have experienced it, as well as those who support them. The book remembers the many parents who have lost children throughout history and chapters weave personal perspectives with the latest research. It examines the experience of sudden deaths, the failures of society in preventing children from dying, the role of social media, how the loss of a child impacts fathers, siblings and relationships, and the usefulness – or otherwise – of bereavement therapies.

A tribute to Reuben's life, this sensitive volume is for those who have experienced loss and want to gain a better understanding of their experience, as well as psychologists, psychotherapists and counsellors working with families.

David Cohen is a prolific writer, filmmaker and psychologist.

The Book of My Son Reuben

A Psychologist on the Loss of His Child

David Cohen

Routledge
Taylor & Francis Group

LONDON AND NEW YORK

Designed cover image: © David Cohen

First published 2023
by Routledge
4 Park Square, Milton Park, Abingdon, Oxon OX14 4RN

and by Routledge
605 Third Avenue, New York, NY 10158

Routledge is an imprint of the Taylor & Francis Group, an informa business

British Library Cataloguing-in-Publication Data
A catalogue record for this book is available from the British Library

ISBN: 978-1-032-22465-7 (hbk)
ISBN: 978-1-032-22464-0 (pbk)
ISBN: 978-1-003-27267-0 (ebk)

DOI: 10.4324/9781003272670

Typeset in Bembo
by Apex CoVantage, LLC

A time to live and a time to die (Ecclesiastes)

Philosophical, poetic and avoids the brutal truth; there is no decent time for a child to die

Contents

17 Reuben – half a life   116

    Extract from *Theo's Ruins* by
    Reuben Cohen (unpublished)   117

    A Brother's Tribute by Nick Cohen   119

    References   121
    Index   133

1 To begin at his end

The cab drives past Liverpool South Parkway Station, past the sign at the roundabout for the Crematorium. Two hundred yards later we got through the entrance to West Allerton Cemetery. The Bishop of Liverpool consecrated the cemetery in September 1909. Of the 75,000 who have been buried here, 5397 were Jewish.

We turn left down a small road and stop by a hedge which surrounds the Jewish cemetery. I have no idea how often I've been here in the last nine years.

I walk onto the grass. Each headstone is decorated with the Star of David. The names are typically Jewish – Steinberg, Kauffman, Zelman, Nettie Olswang, Benmayor, Cohen.

My son now has a headstone Reuben Luke LaTourette Cohen – January 30, 1975–February 9, 2013.

When Leopold Bloom, the "hero" of James Joyce's *Ulysses*, wanders through a Dublin cemetery, he is not impressed by the inscriptions on the gravestones and thinks they should be more specific. "So and So, wheelwright," Bloom imagines, or, on a stone engraved with a saucepan, "I cooked good Irish stew" (2006). Asked to describe ourselves, "Bloom muses, "we might tend to talk in general terms, finding the details of our lives somehow embarrassing." But a friend giving a eulogy would do well to note that we played the guitar, collected antique telephones, loved Agatha Christie and gave a whoop when we did a Killer Sudoko. Details are like a fingerprint.

I wish we had had the imagination to do as Bloom suggested. The book ends with what I wish we had engraved on Reuben's headstone.

The philosopher Simon Blackburn has argued:

> Death can only be thought of as mysterious when we try to understand it by imagining it. And then we will be imagining what it will be like for me. But death is like nothing not because it is mysteriously unlike the things, I have so far known, but because there is no me left.
>
> (Blackburn, 2001)

DOI: 10.4324/9781003272670-1

That is true and not true. Reuben is not alive, but he does exist. I'm not fantasising an afterlife in some celestial bookshop – he loved books – he lives on in our minds, our memories.

Every time I visit these days, I place a stone on the grave. It is well tended. I stand two paces back and say the Kaddish, the Jewish prayer for the dead which heaps blessings on the Almighty without ever mentioning the dead. I don't believe in the Almighty, but rituals soothe a bit. I put a hand on the marble of the grave and say, "Stupid boy." Sometimes I shout it.

Reuben was anything but a stupid boy – except when it came to drugs.

Someone called David Cohen is buried close by. I wonder if I should buy a plot here close to Reuben's. I say, shout, yell his name – as if that would bring him back.

I walk away and turn back to look at his grave again. As if he might suddenly appear out of the ground. I know only too well what lies in the ground.

The bones of the son I loved. He was stocky. His mother said he was a beautiful man, and she is right. His hair was receding a bit, but he was still beautiful.

On my way back to London I wait for a train at Runcorn Station. There is a middle-aged man dressed in black sitting in a wheelchair. He has lost both legs. But he's alive.

Ann Finkbeiner in *The New York Times* (April 21, 2021) reported research from *Up to Date* magazine that doctors suggested that one way to think about grieving is that the feeling of connection to the person who died "gradually moves from preoccupying the mind to residing comfortably in the heart." I'm unsure about that word, "comfortably," it sounds far too cosy. Whatever death is it is not cosy.

This book is not cosy either, but our son and Nick's brother deserves a lasting tribute. Reuben loved books so a book is appropriate. The book tries to integrate three strands. The first is personal and describes Reuben and how we coped – and did not cope – with his death.

The second is historical remembering, the many parents who lost a child and in many cases children. Some historians have argued that in the past children died so frequently parents did not really mourn them. In Victorian London babies were sometimes thrown into the Thames and even sewers. But many parents grieved as desperately, passionately as we do today.

The third strand looks at research. If ever a topic called for sensitive qualitative research, it is this one, but much of the work is quantitative and involves questionnaires with titles like Grief Symptoms Inventory. Then there are academic journals like the *Journal of Bereavement Care* and the award-winning *Funeral Directors Monthly*. Five periodicals cater for what someone is sure to call the undertaker community. I do not apologise for the black humour. Humour is a way of trying to cope with death.

The research raises issues that clutch, and one is: Why can't we make someone we love want to live enough to carry on living? The tragedies described here also force us to try to answer the question: Why do some parents want to kill their defenceless children?

The research has many contradictions, which is not so unusual in psychology. Experiments on how we learn or react to stimuli – How many triangles can you see in nano seconds when you have had a bottle of wine? – produce clear-cut results which may be interesting, but are not the marrow of life.

The book uses a wide variety of sources – historical, research-based and personal accounts. I quote many accounts from parents and siblings who have suffered a loss as they show how complex the way we grieve is.

Perhaps only those who have lived through such a tragedy can begin to understand it. Of the many disturbing questions the book confronts, the most disturbing is: How do those who kill their own children not crumble with guilt but manage to live on?

In 2019 in the UK 1061 babies died – as did 1030 young people aged under 18. In America the death toll is even worse. In the past families might have endured several children dying, but death in childhood is now rare. But still traumatic. Your child dies and you lose not just that person, but your hopes for her or him. Nature has robbed and insulted you. Many parents feel engulfed by grief, but do they have any choice? Can you distract yourself from the sorrow and guilt? Even, should you? I return to this at the end of the book.

Writing any book is a journey – and journeys spring surprises. First, the number of children dying is far greater than I imagined. In 2020 5.0 million children died in the world.

Second, the way official agencies react does not inspire confidence. Since the 1970s, many inquiries into the deaths of children have made sensible recommendations. Experts on social work and medicine have produced thousands of words, which are not much acted on. There are also many examples of utter incompetence on the part of the police. Armed officers cower in doorways as children scream for help and are slaughtered. Why?

Third, I re-discovered the importance of the work of Viktor Frankl, who was ignored by Freud and by way of revenge devised a new form of therapy. For him there are some mundane ways of combatting grief. No need to wheel on the analytic couch. Find a new subject to immerse yourself in. I say re-discovered because when I interviewed him in the late 1970s I was more interested in his spats with Freud than with grief.

Fourth, this is not a self-help book, but it is clear that it is wise to monitor your behaviour when you lose someone. Ask yourself some basic questions:

Do you exercise more? Grief is exhausting. After Reuben died Aileen (Reuben's mother) took walks at 3 am on the beach at New Brighton for months. Exhaustion has its uses. It makes you too tired to cry.

Do you drink more? Men tend to especially.

Do you eat more? Food is comforting. It's no wonder we turn to food to ease the pain of grief. The wake, in Judaism the shiva, is rarely a gourmet feast but sandwiches at least are provided. According to Mrs Beeton, the great Victorian authority on household management, at a proper funeral mourners should be given special biscuits, either shortbread or something like a modern sponge finger. The biscuits were sometimes bundled into parcels and wrapped in paper on which either a poem was printed or drawings of coffins or a skull and cross bones.

Do you smoke more? As there is little research on this, I report my own habit. I smoke four cigars a day now and used to smoke just two.

Do you have difficulties getting up? What after all is the point of carrying on?

Do you feel angry, angry at your husband, wife, children? That's not strange or evil. One of the most disturbing findings reported in this book is that sometimes we feel very aggressive towards those we have lost.

Some sites make one wince. One called Grieve Well offers advice on how to turn death into a chance to grow. It makes me think there should be one called Embrace the Coffin.

As the book weaves between the personal and research it may be helpful to outline its structure:

Chapter 1 "To begin at his end"
Chapter 2 "More about Reuben"
Chapter 3 "Pleasure and panic" looks at how Reuben gave me so much joy and also made me panic.
Chapter 4 "The death of children in antiquity and the Middle Ages" looks at the sad history of families who lost their children – and that includes two great orators - from Cicero to Churchill. Some have found consolation in religion and for an atheist it is well to remember there are millions of Muslims, Catholics and Protestants who believe, as well as those of other faiths.
Chapter 5 looks at the shock of death – the moment you find out, the moment you can never undo.
Chapter 6 When we lost Reuben the world lost a writer. I include some examples of his work.
Chapter 7 looks at how children think about death and how we have tried to comfort ourselves by talking, or thinking we are talking, to our dead.
Chapter 8 – school killings have become almost routine in America. What happens after tragedies like Sandy Hook, Columbine and Uvalde? In every case the killers were young. In virtually every case, the police did not manage the situation well.
Chapter 9 – UK figures from 2016 show that children from poor families were 2.5 times more likely to die young than children from affluent families. The latest figures claimed over 3,300 deaths due to poverty. The chapter looks at the failures of social work in this area.
Chapter 10 "The physical consequences" – what recent neurophysiological science reveals.
Chapter 11 "The psychological research" – the bereaved are supposed to feel denial, anger, bargaining, depression and acceptance, in that order, due to the continuing influence of *On Death and Dying*, the 1969 book

by the psychiatrist Elisabeth Kubler-Ross. However, many, if not most, people will not progress through these stages of grief. The chapter also examines what some now call "complicated grief." Never underestimate the academic capacity to fangle up new syndromes.

Chapter 12 examines the role of social media which sometimes romanticise self-harm and suicide.

Chapter 13 How do couples manage? This chapter examines the impact on marriages.

Chapter 14 looks at how brothers and sisters react to death. Nick has suffered, struggled and written movingly about his brother.

Chapter 15 looks at the research on fathers' reaction to death.

Chapter 16 Can anything be done to help? How useful are bereavement "therapies"?

Chapter 17 "Half a life." Reuben was 38 when he died. What could he have been if he had lived a full life?

There is a Jewish saying "Live long that you may remember long." I intend to remember as long as I can because Reuben does live in my memory.

2   More about Reuben

Some deaths are bitterly cruel. In the 1970s I met Aileen's great aunt Gaby and her husband Jo. They were very proud of their son and drove him to the airport to see him take off. His plane crashed in front of their eyes. Jo's hair turned white in 24 hours. Gaby visited her son's grave every day for years taking food and knitting. She talked to him until eventually someone in the cemetery told her that was enough.

My next experience was also indirect. Reuben went to a Montessori nursery school, which he liked. One of his teachers was a 30-year-old woman who accidentally ran over her little daughter when she was reversing her car. It wrecked the mother's life.

Many parents, who do not have to deal with such a horror, feel guilty about having failed to protect their child. Many experience it as a challenge to basic existential assumptions (Wheeler, 2001). I sometimes do but only sometimes.

I have also had professional experience of untimely death; Reuben worked with Kevin Wells, whose 11-year-old daughter Holly was murdered at Soham by Ian Huntley. Reuben edited Kevin's memoir *Goodbye Dearest Holly* (2001).

Suicides stun parents with even more of a sense of guilt. You think you know your child, but in the aftermath, parents often discover how little they did know. I was frightened Reuben had left a suicide note and was relieved he had not done so. I felt sure that as he loved words, he would have penned one if he had taken his own life.

The pain of not knowing why a child has taken their own life is acute. Gary Speed was credited with setting Wales on the road to the World Cup in 2012. His mother, Carol, has spoken about the sadness that "never goes away," more than a decade after her son took his own life. He was found dead at his home in November 2011.

Carol said something that is repeated by so many parents. She knows she will never find the answer to why he died but urged others to talk about their mental health – and get help. "It's just something that you don't ever get over at all," she said, "You know, you can smile, and you can laugh, and you can have a good day, but it's always there. The sadness is always there."

Aileen has often said you can be cheerful at times but never happy.

DOI: 10.4324/9781003272670-2

Grief is private, public and political. Demonstrations when Palestinian children die – a subject that upset Reuben – are angry and loud. In Anglo-Saxon cultures people do not usually wail or beat their breasts. The pain in our still rather restrained societies is compounded by the feeling that one has not been given "permission" to experience grief dramatically. Imagine howling in a supermarket. People would stare and maybe call security. Restraint involves repression.

Human beings watch and judge each other, so on top of everything else the bereaved are on display. Are you grieving the right way?

Death where is thy sting? Here. Aileen says:

> I'd tend to think you lose the joy and mutuality of that intimacy – exchange it for the terrible intimacy of grief as only you and the person you have lost could really know what it is you have lost – and the bond darkens and changes for sure but speaking for myself does not loosen.

Your children and grandchildren do not make you immortal, but something of you lasts generations into the future.

The psychoanalyst D.W. Winnicott (2021) argued that no parent is, or should try to be, perfect. Being a "good enough" mother is good enough, but you are hardly good enough if your child dies. A parent is supposed to be a competent protector, provider, nurturer. Instead, a child's death imposes social stigma, isolation and, more often than not, loss of social support. Parents also have to find some meaning in life when they don't have the opportunity to help their young grow up.

I am writing when two events highlight the sadness and madness surrounding grief. One is the verdict against Alex Jones whose social media outbursts claimed that the school killings at Sandy Hook in America were fake. No one died, it was all an act. In fact, 20 children and 6 adults died. Jones trumpeted it was part of a conspiracy to tighten gun laws and deny Americans the right to shoot at will. Chapter 8 on school killings returns to this.

My writing also coincides with the inquest into the death of Molly Russell who was 14. On the morning of Molly's death her mother, Janet, said goodbye to one of Molly's sisters who was leaving for school. In a statement at the inquest, read out on her behalf by Oliver Sanders KC, Janet Russell said:

> I knew then something wasn't right. . . . I saw a load of her clothes on the floor (of her bedroom). For some reason I thought Molly had run away. . . . As I looked in her room, I found her . . . I had no doubt it was her.

Janet Russell screamed and ran out of the room. Ian, Molly's father, came upstairs. "I told him not to go into the room, but he did. My other daughter asked 'What's happened?' and I said: 'It's Molly, it's Molly'."

Molly's father, Ian, began giving her CPR while his wife called an ambulance. Paramedics arrived and carried on giving her CPR.

Molly Russell was obsessed with social media and viewed material linked to anxiety, depression, self-harm and suicide before ending her life. Ever since her family has campaigned for better internet safety. A very current issue is whether the algorithms used by social media firms to keep users "hooked" may have contributed to her death. The inquest was delayed in March 2022 after thousands of pages of new evidence about her internet history were submitted to the Coroner.

Her father told the inquest of the "torment" his daughter "must have endured" before her death.

> Five years ago, the Russell family life was unremarkable, yet imperceptibly our adorable youngest family member, Molly, had been struggling with her mental health and hiding her struggles from the rest of us while she battled her demons in the hope of finding peace.

His word "imperceptibly" is terrifying and telling. Carol Speed felt the same sense of not knowing why her son killed himself. Sometimes we only see into each other's minds and souls when it is too late.

A *Times* editorial on October 1, 2022, praised the Coroner Andrew Walker who concluded that the negative effects of social media were partly to blame for Molly's death. He summoned representatives from social media who were defensive. Walker said Meta and Instagram "were seemingly relaxed about carrying obviously harmful material," which often romanticised death as the poet Keats did. Love and death are two eternal poetic themes, so I make no apology for quoting Keats:

> O, for a draught of vintage! that hath been
> > Cool'd a long age in the deep-delved earth,
> Tasting of Flora and the country green,
> > Dance, and Provençal song, and sunburnt mirth!
> O for a beaker full of the warm South,
> > Full of the true, the blushful Hippocrene,
> > > With beaded bubbles winking at the brim,
> > > And purple-stained mouth;
> > That I might drink, and leave the world unseen,
> > > And with thee fade away into the forest dim:
>
> Fade far away, dissolve, and quite forget
> > What thou among the leaves hast never known,
> The weariness, the fever, and the fret
> > Here, where men sit and hear each other groan;
> Where palsy shakes a few, sad, last gray hairs,
> > Where youth grows pale, and spectre-thin, and dies;
> > > Where but to think is to be full of sorrow
> > > And leaden-eyed despairs,
> > Where Beauty cannot keep her lustrous eyes,
> > > Or new Love pine at them beyond to-morrow.
>
> Away! away! for I will fly to thee, . . .
> > (Keats, 1977, "Ode to a Nightingale")

Social media giants claim they are defending free speech, though I have not seen one quote from the French writer Voltaire, author of *Candide* (2006). He said he might disagree with what someone said, but he would defend to the death their right to say it. When it comes to social media giants it is hard not to believe they are also defending their bottom line.

An impossible question. Is it harder to deal with the suicide of a child or murder?

The loss of a child is the loss of promise, potential. A cruel violation of the natural order.

I was there when my son was born and when he died. I loved him, despaired of him, tried to help him.

But not enough.

I have adapted the title from a book by the great French writer, Albert Cohen – *Le livre de ma mère* (2012). It is a touching memoir of his mother who he loved but neglected.

I am alone in the funeral director's side office where Reuben's body has been laid out. A sort of blanket covers him apart from his face. His mother has had her moment alone there. His brother too. Now I stare at what is, alas, a corpse.

Reuben's body is hard, lifeless. His formidable intelligence gone. Give back his being, his brain.

He was a beautiful, quite large baby at almost 8 pounds 9 ounces. It was a quick and easy birth. He was delivered by an aging midwife who was delivering the babies of "her" babies. The attending doctor called him Champagne Charlie, dabbed some champagne on his finger and put it to Reuben's lips.

You don't count how much time you spend with a child, but I spent a lot.

Yet what did I really know about him? Many bereaved parents ask themselves that.

Eight months after his birth Reuben's maternal grandfather died. A brain catastrophe. Reuben's mother became very depressed and blames herself for neglecting him because she was so low. She didn't neglect him, in fact, but she does not seem able to hear that.

So, I try to piece together what I remember.

Reuben wrote and wrote. His one published book *Shooting Reality* (2003) was a history of reality TV written with his friend Sam Brenton. Among Reuben's papers I found a note which pitchforked me. One line said, "I dread my father's return." I always wanted to make him feel good and safe. So how did I make him feel bad?

He could talk the legs off a camel. He was three when I took him to a high-end nursery. He was seen by the head teacher, who was also interviewing another boy; that lad was confused by the experience. Reuben was not. "This is my examination," he said to the delight of the teacher. He was often witty. I was so proud, too proud when I think of it now. I would much rather he was alive now than that he could discuss Nietzsche in detail.

Today as I write it is the eve of Yom Kippur, the Day of Atonement for all Jews. I have much to atone for, too much to ask Reuben to forgive me for.

Reuben's ancestry

Reuben had a complicated background. His mother, Aileen, was American. Her maternal grandparents had a French history. Her grandfather was Irish; his father had been a successful horse rider who once held the record for how high a horse could jump. He married a woman from the small French island of St Pierre et Miquelon off Canada. Grandmère's father was the police chief there and lived into his nineties, perhaps because he drank cognac every day. Aileen's father's parents lived in upstate New York. Her father, William, was a clever student and got to Columbia University before becoming a stockbroker. He drank too much so Reuben did have addiction in his genes. Aileen's mother was energetic but often angry.

My father was Jewish and grew up in Haifa, a town which has a large Arab population. He became a shipping lawyer. He met my mother when he was doing some work for her father who exported coal. My mother, Dolly, was the youngest child of six and remarkably for a woman in the 1930s, she became a lawyer.

She had bad luck with men. She found her first husband in bed with another man, utterly shocking in the 1930s. She then married my father who wanted many children. She did not and had abortions after I was born. He had many mistresses. Religion was some consolation to her. She went to synagogue, and also to church in case God had not decided who the chosen people were.

Dolly liked to make the traditional Jewish Sabbath meal, lighting the candles to mark the start of the day of rest. Reuben liked the ceremony, the blessings on wine and bread and the food. He adored her cheese patties and learned how to make them.

Aileen was not Jewish so, according to Jewish law, Reuben was not Jewish, but he converted to the faith which meant a great deal to him. So, he had a pot pourri of identities. Did they trouble him? I thought not but what did I know?

In their study of 280 families Adcock & Clarke (2011) found that mothers and fathers were hardly brilliant at knowing or guessing the attitudes of their children. Parents made the best guesses on fundamentalist religious beliefs and sexual permissiveness, but being apparently frank about controversial issues did not mean parents had much clue about what their children were thinking.

I don't drive so for years I travelled with Reuben on the school bus with much older boys. I was the only adult. And then we walked from the prep school to the nursery. He didn't mind when he was little. I stopped doing that when he was old enough to go to the prep school.

I can't know what he remembered of me before he died but I know what I most remember.

Reuben was a voracious reader from early childhood. His tastes were not childish. Apart from classics, he was lured by the occult. I did not slap him often; the last time I did so was when he was ten and found he had created a shrine to Aleister Crowley, the vicious "master" of the dark arts. The *Daily*

Mail called Crowley the wickedest man on earth. He was suspected of killing a baby among many other atrocities. I was terrified by Reuben's fascination with the man. I made him dismantle the "altar" and tried to make him see why Crowley was evil.

One of the factors that made us blind was the rather devious behaviour of my mother who was depressed herself. When he bunked off school in his early teens, he went to her flat in the West End and she took him to lunch. She did not tell me or his mother. He also saw that she took many tranquillisers. He tried some for himself, from her supply. He loved her. He did not find loving hard.

Aileen and I both worked so we found a helper from the Quaker meeting Aileen sometimes attended. The girl was impatient with him and shouted at him. They got along very badly.

Reuben left Alleyn's School when he was 16. A wise teacher suggested he should move to a college of further education. He loved it there and got great A levels which got him to Oxford. He hated Oxford though. He made a suicide attempt the full truth of which neither I nor his mother ever knew. His brother saved him.

Reuben left Oxford and wanted to go to the States. It suited me because I asked him to help me research a book on Carl Rogers, the founder of humanistic psychotherapy. Reuben did the research brilliantly and though I acknowledged his work fulsomely, the book was a source of tension between us.

His stay in the States led him to write a fine novel, *Theo's Ruins*. It was never published. There was also a very playful side to him and his writings. He also landed in jail for drug use but his great aunt, a formidable lawyer, got him out.

He came back and went to Sussex University. By then I had separated from Aileen and was living with Julia. We took him to his digs. Sussex, like so many universities, was a haven for drugs. Reuben tried to cure himself going on the Twelve Steps programme, but never managed it entirely. Neither I nor his mother gave him an ultimatum. We did not manage tough love, though who knows if that cliché would have worked.

Reuben loved Sussex. He had good friends including Becky and Josh who had two children. Reuben spent much time with them especially after Becky developed cancer. She was 26 when she died. He missed her badly.

Reuben attracted girls and went to Vietnam with one. She was damaged herself. There had been a murder in her family. He was drawn to difficult women. One was a poet who had left her children. Aileen warned him that he should not trust a woman who did that, but he did not listen. Another woman had been a sex worker. I disliked her but he got engaged to her. Aileen went to the States to see them, but the woman wanted Reuben to keep taking drugs. Reuben had begun a serious relationship that came out of a long friendship but he had doubts as to whether he could or should cope with a relationship and worried about its effect on the other person. But he was hopeful and spoke to her on the last day of his life, planning to spend time with her soon.

He got a good degree and came back to London. He took a flat with a friend but that didn't last. He became a temp and worked for the Post Office. He then got a job doing publicity for books and, later, as the assistant to my literary agent, Sonia Land.

I was often anxious when we agreed to meet, and sometimes he was late. I paced up and down outside Waterstones in Piccadilly once. I finally rang my half-brother, Daniel. Reuben was staying in a flat Daniel rented out to him. He was zonked out, Daniel said. An hour or so later Reuben rang me, groggy, apologetic. I was just relieved to hear his voice.

Then, I paid for a teaching English as a Foreign Language (EFL) course. Coming home one day round lunch time I met Reuben going into our house. He hated EFL. He was sorry. He was sorry I'd wasted the money on the course. I was angry as it had been hard to find the cash at that time, but even more worried than angry.

Julia, with whom I was living, and Reuben liked each other at first. She took a splendid photo of him up the stairs. He often got her to give him £20 or £10. But his feelings changed and for many years he did not speak to her.

Julia's husband died when her children Alex and Katy were young, so Reuben's death also brought back painful memories of that for them. I have to say that Reuben and they fell out and he stopped speaking to them, too.

Then came one of those strange coincidences. ITV commissioned me to make a film about the murders of Holly Wells and Jessica Chapman at Soham. Kevin, Holly's father, had failed to get the diary that he wrote to keep sane in the wake of her murder published. I agreed to publish the book and asked Reuben to work with Kevin on the text. They got on well. I weave in some comparisons between Kevin's reactions and mine 11 years later.

Ironically the book became a best-seller.

Sons bargain with fathers so when the book got to 6 in the UK best-seller list, I paid Reuben £20000. It was fair but I fear much of it bought drugs.

The book opened up a new career for Reuben. I had begun to work with a rich man. I'll call him M. Reuben persuaded him to put up the money to start a small publishing company. For three years Reuben was its editorial director. He published many books including a follow up to the 1970s best-seller *Sucking Sherbet Lemons* by Michael Carson. I filmed an interview Reuben did with the author. Precious now. He found some good books like *Murder at the Blue Parrot* which had no literary pretensions.

Then the publishing business went wrong. M wanted to have a real hit or to make money. After over three years we had had neither a best-seller nor a critical success. M sacked Reuben. Though he had been very ambivalent about M and hated what he saw as me deferring to him, which I did partly to keep M sweet so he would keep employing Reuben.

When I told M Reuben had died, he emailed me "Have a hug." It made me angry at the time but then it is rare for people to respond "well" to a death.

After that Reuben worked as an editor for Jeremy Robson and worked on *The Boxer*, a story of a Jewish fighter. We also discussed him writing a book on Freud and his use of cocaine. Reuben insisted I write it, however, as I had written a book on how Freud escaped Vienna in 1938 with the help of a decent Nazi. Reuben came up with a brilliant opening that compared the drug experiences of Freud and William Burroughs. They were similar except for the fact that Freud gave up cocaine after 20 years and turned to cigars. Burroughs never gave up drugs.

In the year before he died Reuben was living in Norbury where he had a flat in a house that belonged to my father's second wife, Evi. You had to negotiate to visit him. A favour he rarely granted. His living room was littered with bottles. I didn't do what I should have done and insisted on him cleaning it up.

Then he went to live with his mother near Liverpool.

They did for a while, and I went to visit them sometimes. There is a Phoenix House a few miles from Aileen's house. Phoenix House takes addicts in and offers a setting in which they can stop using drugs. To my shame we did not insist on Reuben going to visit it.

Of course, I remember more about Reuben, but each memory is painful. I had not managed to keep him alive. There is no curse worse than the death of your child.

If I've learned anything it is that grief is very individual. Some approaches strike me as too academic, especially the theory of five stages of grief and the more recent development of "complicated grief."

I have said that I have sometimes used humour to make pain less painful. In my *Home Alone* (2013) I described how my parents left me and the pain and terror I felt; readers commented on the fact that I hadn't lost my sense of humour. It is impossible to find that when your child dies.

3 Pleasure and panic

I have many fond memories of Reuben on holiday. When he was two and a bit, Aileen and I took a villa in Crete. There is a lovely photo of him stark naked coming down the stairs. He also liked Istanbul where we spent a holiday in a flat belonging to my aunt and uncle.

We sometimes went to Wetherspoons to have a cheap lunch.

We occasionally walked through Greenwich Park on the way to his nursery. When he was seven or, so Reuben started to go to a karate class in Covent Garden. Ian, the teacher or *sensei*, encouraged him and for a while Reuben was keen. He got a brown belt. It was the only sport he ever had any interest in.

In his twenties he lived with his brother for a while near Herne Hill. His room at the back had a small balcony so he could go out there to smoke. He was a devoted smoker. We sometimes went to cigar shops – I smoke them – and I bought him whatever brand he fancied. Whenever I went abroad, I brought him back a carton of cigarettes.

He liked my mother's flat in Seymour Place where she made Friday night dinners he loved.

His aunt Amelie and her husband Ralph had a house in Falmouth near Cape Cod. They had a small lake at the bottom of their garden, and we went canoeing on it together. Fun, it was always fun when we were doing something calm together.

Reuben was worried about the state of Israel and the deaths of Palestinians. We went to Israel together and visited Mount Carmel where I was born and the magnificent Bahai Gardens.

Among the many pictures of him there are a few particular favourites – one when he was three and standing with his brother in our garden, one of him in a yellow raincoat, one of him wearing a diving mask and a later one of him playing with snow. He is smiling. Pictures of him after he was 15 do not show him smiling much.

Julia and I bought a house in Oakley Square and Reuben had a room in the basement. He liked it and later made something of a cave in a house Julia and I had in East Road.

DOI: 10.4324/9781003272670-3

He liked synagogues too. For a while he went to *heder*, Sunday school at the grand synagogue in Seymour Place which my mother attended. He then changed to a more radical one in Montagu Street in London's West End.

Later I took Reuben to Rhodes for Easter. I have a picture of him reading a book on his bed. The trip did not go well but that had nothing to do with Reuben. The hotel was rude, and we left it.

Then when I had been commissioned to make a film on mental health worldwide, I took him and Nicholas to Japan with me. We spent some time on the Izu peninsula outside Tokyo. The boys loved it. Nicholas who was 15 showed all the social skills he had acquired. Reuben also loved Japan. I thought we should go to Hiroshima. We took the bullet train and walked in the Peace Memorial Park.

As well as reading Reuben loved music. Aileen remembers taking him to hear Thea Gilmore. He also liked to cook. After we came back from Japan, he started to cook Japanese dishes. He once cooked a delicious Japanese meat stew. He loved cooking spaghetti bolognaise and during the time when he felt very Jewish, he kept some of the kosher rules. At Christmas he made a stew with chestnuts.

He read avidly. Dostoevsky was a particular favourite. So was William Burroughs and the sociologist Studs Terkel who dissected the divisions in American society.

But from the time he was 13 drugs were ever present. Neither his mother nor I took enough notice of the risks he was running – and we did not confront him when we should have done. In her novel *Oh William!* (2022) Elisabeth Strout points out we are all mysterious to others – and even to ourselves. Goethe (2015), Freud's favourite author, wrote "If I knew myself, I'd run away."

I should have been alert as my ITV film *Kicking the Habit* followed how addicts did or did not recover. I did not use what I knew to help my son.

4 The death of children in antiquity and the Middle Ages

The Romans could sell their children and even kill them until a law in the fourth century outlawed that. Romans did not consider children as beings who had a soul. So, they often discarded dead infants or buried them in the garden like a dead dog.

Infanticide was common. Women were allowed to dispose of their children if they wanted to. Boys were more highly valued than girls, but archaeological sites suggest both sexes were killed equally. A child only became "human" when he or she reached certain milestones like naming, teething and eating solid foods.

Fathers held the power of life or death. After birth, the baby was placed at the father's feet. If the father picked it up, the child stayed at home. Otherwise, it was abandoned outside for anyone to pick up – or to die of exposure. Roman infants were often rejected if they were born deformed, a daughter or the family could not afford to support another child. The lucky ones were adopted by childless couples and received the family's name. But there were many unlucky ones and they risked being sold as slaves or prostitutes or being maimed by beggars; maimed children got more sympathy – and the beggar more money.

Being a Roman child seems to have been a risky business. The evidence is contradictory, however, as the epitaphs composed for infant tombs also often reveal the intense, quite modern, love and grief parents felt. One inscription read that the baby's life consisted of just "nine breaths." In another a father wrote:

> My baby Aceva was snatched away to live in Hades before she had her fill of the sweet light of life. She was beautiful and charming, a little darling as if from heaven, her father weeps for her and, because he is her father, asks that the earth may rest lightly on her forever.

The most notable example of a loving Roman father is Cicero.

Cicero

Tullia, Cicero's daughter, was his first child and married Gaius Calupurnius Piso Fruge in 63 BCE when they were both teenagers. Piso died three years

DOI: 10.4324/9781003272670-4

later, after which Tullia married Furius Crassipes. Cicero doted on Tullia and once complained to her mother that she had not equipped her daughter with enough money and an escort for the journey to see him.

In 50 BCE Tullia married Publius Cornelius Dolabella, with whom she had two children. The first son was born in May 49 BCE but died the same year. The second was born in February 45 BCE and survived but complications during childbirth led to Tullia's death.

Plutarch wrote:

> His friends came together from all quarters to comfort Cicero; but his grief at his misfortune was excessive, so that he actually divorced the wife he had wedded, because she was thought to be pleased at the death of Tullia.
>
> (Plutarch, *Cicero*, 1919)

Sixteen centuries later the feelings of loss are just as raw.

Shakespeare lost his only son Hamnet when the boy was 11 years old. He could not bear to use his name as a character, so Hamnet became Hamlet. Early in the play the ghost of Hamlet's father warns his son that he was murdered by his brother who went on to marry Gertrude, Hamlet's mother. No wonder Freud liked the play, and his biographer Ernest Jones wrote a long paper about it.

Shakespeare's contemporary Ben Jonson, who wrote that sly comedy, *Volpone*, also lost his son and wrote:

> On my first son
>
> Farewell, thou child of my right hand, and joy;
> My sin was too much hope of thee, lov'd boy.
> Seven years tho' wert lent to me, and I thee pay,
> Exacted by thy fate, on the just day.
> O, could I lose all father now! For why
> Will man lament the state he should envy?
> To have so soon 'scap'd world's and flesh's rage,
> And if no other misery, yet age?
> Rest in soft peace, and, ask'd, say, "Here doth lie
> Ben Jonson his best piece of poetry."
> For whose sake henceforth all his vows be such,
> As what he loves may never like too much.
>
> (Jonson, 2021, "On My First Son")

John Evelyn

"Here ends the joy of my life" – the diary entry of John Evelyn recorded after his son Richard died on January 27, 1658. Evelyn described the "inexpressible grief and affliction" that he and his wife Mary suffered. Richard was their first-born child "5 years and 3 days old onely, but at that tender age a prodigy for witt and understanding; for beauty of body a very angel; for endowment of mind of incredible and rare hopes" (Evelyn, 2006). This was not last tragedy for the couple.

On March 7, 1685, Evelyn wrote,

> My daughter Mary aged 19 was taken with the smallpox. She had visited a house where a maid had smallpox, but no one warned visitors. . . . Soon there was found to be no hope. She died on the 14th to our unspeakable sorrow.

Evelyn gave a fetching pen portrait of his daughter. She read the classics and "She was a little miracle" (Evelyn, 2006).

Of the eight children the Evelyns had, seven died. Yet the Evelyns continued living. Some parents fared even worse.

Queen Anne

The film *The Favourite* (2018) showed how Queen Anne was pregnant at least 17 times and miscarried or gave birth to stillborn children at least 12 times. Of her five liveborn children, four died before the age of two.

When her son William was born, he was weak and few believed he would live long. His first wet nurse had too large a nipple, so she was replaced. William suffered from "an issue from his pole," according to his servant Lewis Jenkin, who wrote a touching memoir of the boy. A pole suggests he had some fluid coming from his brain. However, William developed normally. He played games with soldiers and organised a troop of boys to play at war games. He looked forward to becoming king.

In July 1700, however, William became very ill and died after suffering a high fever for five days. His death meant Anne had no heir. The Stuart dynasty was at an end. Anne and her husband were "overwhelmed with grief." Anne ordered her household to observe a day of mourning every year on the anniversary of his death.

Being a genius was no safeguard either.

Charles Darwin

Most biographers agree Darwin came up with his theory of the evolution of species when he was under 30. And yet, he did not publish it for another 21 years. This leaves many asking why he waited – and for so long.

Darwin's wife, Emma Wedgewood, was a devout Christian who was upset by her husband's lack of faith. Some biographers claim that facing the death of their oldest daughter, Annie, in particular, gave Darwin deeper insight into the nature of evolution and helped Emma come to terms with her husband's work.

When Darwin married Emma, she told him she wanted to love and be with him forever. And "forever," for Emma, meant beyond "till death do us part."

Emma knew her husband had doubts about the orthodoxies of religion and worried that his scientific investigations would only deepen his doubts, therefore she would be condemned to living alone for an eternity. And she told him so, biographers say.

So, Darwin waited and worried and waited.

Then the story took a tragic turn. The Darwins' beloved oldest daughter, Annie, died just after turning ten. Darwin was so overcome with grief that he could not go to her burial.

There is a paradox. Death can be a spur. After Annie died, Darwin became more willing to proclaim his theories – and his religious doubts. While still keeping her faith, Emma turned towards Darwin, not away from him.

Lyanda Haupt, one of many writers on Darwin, says one can see the influence of Annie's death in his shaping of *On the Origin of Species* (1859). "He knew so deeply and so personally and viscerally what death was now after Annie's loss," Haupt says. And, yet, in his writing "you see him affirming over and over this circle, the endless unfolding of life" (Haupt, 2006).

In the last pages of *On the Origin of Species*, Darwin takes his readers to a beautiful forest, rich with trees and birds singing everywhere, and reminds us of the beauty we see every day, in things like butterflies and flowers. And he stresses, especially, that humans, who can contemplate and love these things, are all products of millions of years of competition, struggle, famine and death – and that this struggle will continue. So, life will keep evolving new forms and new shapes.

He is saying there are two things that are true: one is that everything dies, and things die for no reason and to no apparent end. And their death is painful. And, the other is that the process of living and dying produces something amazing and beautiful and astonishing.

Darwin himself wrote, "There is grandeur in this view of life . . . from so simple a beginning, endless forms most beautiful and most wonderful have been, and are being, evolved" (Darwin, 1859).

The First World War made the death of children all too familiar. The son of the English writer Rudyard Kipling, John, went missing in action at the Battle of Loos, on September 27, 1915. The 18-year-old lieutenant became the most widely searched-for soldier of the war. His desperate father mobilised every resource he could. The Prince of Wales, the Crown Princess of Sweden and the American Ambassador in London all tried to help. The Royal Flying Corps dropped mimeographed sheets behind enemy lines in case someone had found the son alive or his body.

Kipling and his wife visited war hospitals and interviewed soldiers from John's regiment, the Irish Guards, hoping for a scrap of information. In his poem, "My boy Jack," Kipling lay bare his agony.

My boy Jack
"Have you news of my boy Jack?"
Not this tide.

> "When d'you think that he'll come back?"
> *Not with this wind blowing, and this tide.*
> "Has any one else had word of him?"
> *Not this tide.*
> *For what is sunk will hardly swim,*
> *Not with this wind blowing, and this tide.*
> "Oh, dear, what comfort can I find?"
> *None this tide,*
> *Nor any tide,*
> *Except he did not shame his kind—*
> *Not even with that wind blowing, and that tide.*
> *Then hold your head up all the more,*
> *This tide,*
> *And every tide;*
> *Because he was the son you bore,*
> *And gave to that wind blowing and that tide!*
>   (Kipling, 1994, "My Boy Jack")

Finally in 1992, John's remains were found in Chalk Pit Wood – though there is still some doubt about that claim. Kipling wrote:

> That flesh we had nursed from the first in all cleanness was given . . .
> To be blanched or gay-painted by fumes – to be cindered by fires –
> To be senselessly tossed and retossed in stale mutilation
> From crater to crater. For this we shall take expiation.
> *But who shall return us our children?*
>   (Kipling, 1994, "The Children")

In memory of his son Kipling wrote the history of the Irish Guards, which took seven years and left him, according to his wife's diary, "yellow and shrunken." Still, he trudged on stoically with his public duties: Red Cross work, visiting the wounded, touring the front, writing poems and stories. Stoicism, after all, was the keystone of "If," the manifesto of manliness dedicated to John, which has been repeatedly voted Britain's most beloved poem. But just as "If" was written for John, so too, in a case of surpassingly bitter symmetry, was Kipling's other landmark poem that also opened with that title word:

> If any question why we died,
> Tell them, because our fathers lied.
>   (Kipling, 1994, "Epitaphs of War")

John was the second child whom the Kiplings had lost. Their six-year-old daughter, Josephine, for whom the stories in *The Jungle Book* (1894) were written, had died of pneumonia in New York in 1899.

Sigmund Freud

Sigmund Freud's two sons served in the Austrian Army in the First World War – and survived. He discussed death in his paper *Mourning and Melancholia* (1957[1915]) arguing, "although mourning involves grave departures from the normal attitude to life, it never occurs to us to regard it as a pathological condition."

One of Freud's close associates Abraham (1988[1912]) said of mourning:

> We rely on its being overcome after a certain lapse of time, and we look upon any interference with it as useless or even harmful. The distinguishing mental features of melancholia are a profoundly painful dejection, cessation of interest in the outside world, loss of the capacity to love, inhibition of all activity, and a lowering of the self-regarding feelings to a degree that finds utterance in self-reproaches and self-revilings and culminates in a delusional expectation of punishment. This picture becomes a little more intelligible when we consider that, with one exception, the same traits are met with in mourning.

Freud then claimed: "The disturbance of self-regard is absent in mourning" (1957[1915]). A recent paper suggests that is not always the case. Charlotte Angelhoff, Josefin Sveen, Anette Alvariza, Megan Weber-Falk and Ulrika Kreicbergs (2021) argue not only that talking and grieving together may help belief in a meaningful future and can help bereaved adolescents and their parents. Their study explored communication, self-esteem and prolonged grief in adolescent-parent dyads, following the death of a parent to cancer. Twenty families completed the Rosenberg Self-Esteem Scale and Prolonged Grief-13, 1–4 years following the death of a parent, among other questionnaires. Angelhoff et al. found self-esteem has a strong relation to happiness. Although the research has not clearly established causation, they argue that high self-esteem does lead to greater happiness. Also low self-esteem is more likely than high to lead to depression under some circumstances. Some studies maintain that high self-esteem mitigates the effects of stress, but other studies come to the opposite conclusion, indicating that the negative effects of low self-esteem are mainly felt in good times. Still others find that high self-esteem leads to happier outcomes regardless of stress or other circumstances.

Eleven children and their remaining parent said they had normal to high self-esteem.

In his paper Freud went on,

> but otherwise the features are the same. Profound mourning, the reaction to the loss of someone who is loved, contains the same painful frame of mind, the same loss of interest in the outside world – in so far as it does not recall him – the same loss of capacity to adopt any new object of love

(which would mean replacing him) and the same turning away from any activity that is not connected with thoughts of him.

(Freud, 1957[1915])

Despite the point about self-esteem, as ever Freud's description was accurate. He continued:

We shall probably see the justification for this when we are in a position to give a characterization of the economics of pain. In what, now, does the work which mourning performs consist of? I do not think there is anything far-fetched in presenting it in the following way. Reality-testing has shown that the loved object no longer exists, and it proceeds to demand that all libido shall be withdrawn from its attachments to that object.

(Freud, 1957[1915])

To grieve is normal. To be melancholic or depressed is not. Mourning consumes you. You lose the will to live. Freud wrote:

In mourning it is the world which has become poor and empty; in melancholia it is the ego itself. The patient represents his ego to us as worthless, incapable of any achievement and morally despicable; he reproaches himself, vilifies himself and expects to be cast out and punished.

(Freud, 1957[1915])

Freud stressed the impact of grief:

what is psychologically very remarkable – by an overcoming of the instinct which compels every living thing to cling to life. It would be equally fruitless from a scientific and a therapeutic point of view to contradict a patient who brings these accusations against his ego.

(Freud, 1957[1915])

When Freud's daughter, Sophie, died, the reality of his grief was very different from his theoretical model. In a condolence letter to a friend, nine years after Sophie's death, he wrote:

Although we know that after such a loss the acute stage of mourning will subside, we also know we shall remain inconsolable and will never find a substitute. No matter what may fill the gap, even if it be filled completely, it nevertheless remains something else. Actually, this is how it should be. It is the only way of perpetuating that love which we do not wish to relinquish.

(Freud, 1957[1915])

Freud's letter to a friend about her death described this eloquently:

> For years I was prepared for the loss of my sons (in war); and now comes
> that of my daughter. Since I am profoundly irreligious there is no one
> I can accuse, and I know there is nowhere to which any complaint could
> be addressed. "The unvarying circle of a soldier's duties" and the "sweet
> habit of existence" will see to it that things go on as before. Quite deep
> down I can trace the feelings of a deep narcissistic hurt that is not to be
> healed.
>
> (Freud, 1957[1915])

As stated, loss can spur the bereaved to work. After Sophie died, Freud developed the death instinct, the opposite of the pleasure principle.

Early in his research Freud developed the concept of the *pleasure principle*,
because an organism avoids harm to preserve and perpetuate life. During the
First World War, Freud observed that some people who returned from war
would relive the traumatic events or dream of the events related to their trauma,
a phenomenon he termed *repetition compulsion*. Freud also noticed his grandson
did something similar when his parents went away; the boy would re-enact the
disappearance and reappearance of his parents and himself as time passed in a
theatre-like performance while in his crib. This puzzled Freud, who noticed
his patients would relive unsettling events and patterns in their lives, despite
finding these repetition compulsions harmful or unpleasant. This went against
the pleasure principle, so Freud, being ever curious, sought another explanation
for his observations; he developed the idea of the death instinct, *thanatos*, later
in his life because of these phenomena.

In *Why War,* a pamphlet he wrote with Einstein in 1932, the two were hoping to prevent war:

> After years of listening to human
> misery, I don't believe that in some
> happy corner of the earth there are
> races who live without being
> aggressive. If I'm wrong, please send
> me the address of these happy folk.
>
> We may become slowly intelligent
> enough to avoid conflict as war runs
> counter to the psychic disposition
> imposed on us by the growth of
> culture.

But Freud doubted it.

Sibelius

The Finnish composer lost his youngest daughter, Kirsti, in February 1900. He became depressed and took to excessive drinking. It did not stop him working though. He rewrote his first symphony and went on an international tour which made his international reputation.

Winston Churchill

Marigold Churchill was just 2 years and 9 months old when she died of septicaemia. She was buried in a quiet and simple grave in London. Winston Churchill wrote the year of her death affected him "grievously." The pain stayed with him all his life. Two years before he died his daughter Diana committed suicide. He saved the world but could not keep all his children alive.

President Biden

President Biden has had to face the horrors of loss often.

> Was it something in the way Val's voice caught? . . . What I felt was something jarring, something stronger than a premonition. It was a physical sensation, like a little pinprick at the centre of my chest. I could already feel Neilia's absence. "She's dead," I said, isn't she?"
>
> (Biden, 2021)

His 13-month-old daughter, Naomi, was also killed in the automobile accident. His sons, Beau and Hunter, who were three and four, respectively, were injured but survived. Biden added that suicide was not just an option but

> a rational option. But I'd look at Beau and Hunter asleep and wonder what new terrors their own dreams held and wonder who would explain to my sons my being gone too. And I knew I had no choice but to fight to stay alive.
>
> (Biden, 2021)

Then, in 2015, when he was 46, Beau, a decorated war veteran and Delaware's attorney general, lost his battle with brain cancer.

In his *Super Soul Sunday* conversation with Oprah (2017), Biden said the loss of his son is still something he is struggling to come to terms with (Biden, 2021).

> I sometimes find myself – say something about him, and I can't handle it. I start to break down. So, it's not like the pain ever goes away. But what I do is I look at my grandson, his son, and I see him. I look at my granddaughter. I see her. And I know he's still here. I know he's still with me.

As a film maker I recorded a dramatic example of witnessing death being an inspiration to action. In 1977 Moluccan terrorists captured a Dutch train. I made *After the Hijack* (1977), a film for ITV about what happened to the hostages. Jan Bastiaans, Holland's leading psychiatrist, claimed all of them would be traumatised; indeed, some were. However, two found it changed their lives positively. Hans Prins, a biologist, and Gerhard Vaders, the editor of north Holland's leading paper, were on the train. They tried to negotiate a compromise. They failed at first but became convinced the terrorists had reasons for their action. The Dutch had abandoned the Moluccan islands to Indonesia and promised to return them to the Moluccans. Prins and Vaders became advocates for their cause.

The Compassionate Friends

As this book often deals with volunteers, it is useful to explain the origins of one of their most famous organisations. The Compassionate Friends was founded in 1969 by Joe and Iris Lawley, whose son, Kenneth, was killed in a road traffic accident, and Bill and Joan Henderson, whose son, Billy, died from cancer, both in May 1968.

Joe Lawley's family were dealing with the usual early morning hassle as they washed, dressed, ate and finally shared a moment as the children left for school. He wrote:

> We were four – Iris and Joe, parents, Angela (the elder of our children, aged nearly fifteen) and Kenneth – the younger, nearly twelve. The youngsters departed and then, minutes later, as we prepared to leave too, the telephone rang. I picked it up, a voice said, "There's been an accident. Kenneth has been taken to hospital by ambulance." We rushed to the hospital convincing each other that it could be nothing worse than a broken limb, but within a short time we knew that it was serious, he was unconscious; later we were told that he had suffered major head injuries, with resultant brain damage. We were face-to-face with death.
>
> (The Compassionate Friends, Mission Statement)

Elsewhere in the hospital, Billy Henderson's parents had nursed him through a long illness, at his bedside day and night. The Henderson family and the Lawleys were all known to the Rev. David Dale, a minister in the United Reformed Church.

Standing back from the relatives and friends round Kenneth's bed in the Intensive Care Unit was another young man in clerical garb, the Reverend Simon Stephens. He simply said, "If I can help . . . I am here, all of the time." Eventually we asked, "Will you pray for Kenneth and when he did so, he mentioned Billy Henderson." Prayer did not save the boy.

Joe Lawley wrote,

> Iris suggested that we send flowers to Joan and Bill; we did not then know the significance of that act, but looking back, it might be said that The Compassionate Friends started there. Joan and Bill telephoned their thanks and we met for a cup of tea . . . Together, midst freely flowing tears, the four of us were able for the first time to speak openly of our children, without feelings of guilt that we were endlessly repeating the virtues of our children, and of our vanished hopes for the future. Together, we were all able to accept, for the first time, the words used by many well-meaning friends – rejected almost universally by parents who have lost a beloved child – "I understand". *We did understand, all four of us, and*, in the immensity of our grief (and in reality, is there any other tragedy of quite this enormity?), we all suffered together.
>
> We were helping each other – a telephone call in the blackest hour brought love and help immediately to the door.

The Compassionate Friends

> aims to help anyone affected by the death of a child, including unmarried partners, adoptive parents, stepfamilies, same sex couples and single parent families. It has no religious affiliation and offers support to bereaved families irrespective of the age of the child, cause of death, ethnic, social or political background.
>
> (The Compassionate Friends, Mission Statement)

They have rarely had to deal with death in war though.

In 1982 David Grossman, the famous Israeli writer, publicly urged his government to accept a ceasefire. Just days later, his soldier son was killed by one of Hezbollah's final anti-tank missiles. The following is the eulogy Grossman read at the funeral:

> At 20 to three in the morning, between Saturday and Sunday, the doorbell rang. Over the intercom, they said they were from the army. For three days, every thought begins with: 'He/we won't"
>
> He won't come. We won't talk. We won't laugh. He won't be that kid with the ironic look in his eyes and the amazing sense of humour. He won't be that young person with understanding deeper than his years. There won't be that warm smile and healthy appetite. There won't be that rare combination of determination and gentleness. There won't be his common sense and wisdom. We won't sit down together to watch *The Simpsons* and *Seinfeld*, and we won't listen to Johnny Cash, and we won't feel the strong embrace. We won't see you going to talk to your brother, Yonatan, with excited hand movements and we won't see you hugging your sister, Ruthie, the love of your life.

Uri, my love. All your short life, we have all learned from you, from the strength and determination to go your own way. To go your own way even if there is no way you could succeed. We followed with amazement your struggle to get into the tank commanders' course. How you never compromised with your commanders, because you knew you would be a great commander. You were not satisfied to give less than you thought you could. And when you succeeded, I thought here's a man who knows his own abilities in such a simple and wise way. Here's a man who has no pretensions or arrogance, who isn't influenced by what others say about him, whose source of strength is internal.

From childhood, you were like that. A child who lived in harmony with himself and those around him. A child who knew his place, and knew that he was loved, who recognised his limitations and strengths. And truly, from the moment you forced the army to make you a commander, it was clear what kind of commander and person you were. We hear today from your comrades and your subordinates about the commander and friend. About the person who got up before everyone else in order to organise every-thing and who went to sleep only after everyone else had. And yesterday, at midnight, I looked at our house which was quite a mess after the visits of hundreds of people who came to console us and I said to myself: 'Well, now we need Uri, to help us organise it again.'

You were the leftie of your battalion, and you were respected for it, because you stood your ground, without giving up even one of your mili-tary assignments . . .

You were a son and a friend to me and to Mummy. Our soul is tied to yours. You felt good in yourself, and you were a good person to live with. I cannot even say out loud how much you were 'Someone to Run With'. Every furlough you would say: 'Dad, let's talk' and we would go, usually to a restaurant, and talk. You told me so much, Uri, and I felt proud that I was your confidante.

I won't say anything now about the war you were killed in. We, our family, have already lost in this war. The state of Israel will have its own reckoning . . .

Uri was such an Israeli child; even his name was very Israeli and Hebrew. He was the essence of Israeli-ness as I would want it to be. An Israeli-ness that has almost been forgotten, that is something of a curiosity. And he was a person so full of values. That word has been so eroded and has become ridiculed in recent years. In our crazy, cruel and cynical world, it's not 'cool' to have values, or to be a humanist, or to be truly sensitive to the suffering of the other, even if that other is your enemy on the battlefield.

However, I learned from Uri that it is both possible and necessary to be all that. We have to guard ourselves, by defending ourselves both physically and morally. We have to guard ourselves from might and simplistic think-ing, from the corruption that is in cynicism, from the pollution of the heart and the ill-treatment of humans, which are the biggest curse of those living in a disastrous region like ours. Uri simply had the courage to be himself, always and in all situations – to find his exact voice in everything he said and did. That's what guarded him from the pollution and corruption and the diminishing of the soul.

In the night between Saturday and Sunday, at 20 to three in the morning, our doorbell rang. The person said through the intercom that he was from the army, and I went down to open the door, and I thought to myself – that's it, life's over. But five hours later, when Michal and I went into Ruthie's room to wake her and tell her the terrible news, Ruthie, after first crying, said: 'But we will live, right? We will live and trek like before and I want to continue singing in a choir, and we will continue to laugh like always and I want to learn to play guitar.' And we hugged her and told her that we will live.

We will derive our strength from Uri; he had enough for many years to come. Vitality, warmth and love radiated from him strongly, and that will shine on us even if the star that made it has been extinguished. Our love, we had a great honour to live with you. Thank you for every moment that you were ours.

Father and Mother, Yonatan and Ruthie
(Translated from the original Hebrew by Joseph Millis,
world news editor of the *Jewish Chronicle*)

The roll call of the dead young is long, a black banner of too short lives. Two hundred and fifty years earlier the poet Chatterton was broke and killed himself. So did John Polidori who wrote the first Vampire story in 1819.

Kurt Cobain, Janis Joplin and Amy Whitehouse are also part of that "tradition." These rock stars had everything going for them. So why again, why did they kill themselves?

Victor Frankl

I have been writing about psychology for 50 years and interviewed many famous psychologists. When he was very young Viktor Frankl sent one of his papers to Freud who did not bother to reply. That slight prompted Frankl to devise a theory which was critical of Freud. Frankl became famous for the book he wrote after being in Auschwitz; although he did not address the death of children directly, he discussed what helps you survive in extreme circumstances. He told me that

> what is more crucial than anything in affecting the chances of survival in such extreme circumstances is the orientation a person has to his future. Is there a goal, a meaning waiting in the future for you to be fulfilled exclusively by you?

(Frankl, 1978)

Frankl said he had always argued:

> there are three ways to meaning. One is creative one is experiential; one is attitudinal. You can achieve meaning by creating a work or doing a deed. You can achieve meaning by experiencing something good and true in nature or culture or, indeed, by experiencing someone in his person hood which means loving him. And thirdly by your attitude.
>
> (Frankl, 1978)

Frankl went on to argue that even if fate placed you in a vice you could not change, but "you may submit and try inwardly to overcome it by your hero-ism." How can you deal with the trauma "in a worthy way?"

For bereaved parents finding any such meaning is hard indeed.

5 The shock of death

Reuben celebrated his thirty-eighth birthday nine days before he died. I rushed up to his room in New Brighton.

Reuben was sitting in his chair in his room.

I walked up to him. He did not move.

I shouted his name. He did not respond.

He was dead.

In those days 999 replied quickly. The paramedics hovered round him for no more than a minute.

They phoned the police who were there fast. The police at first refused to let us stay by his body. We argued and they relented. We waited for the paramedics to do something, thump his chest, inject him, anything but no he had been dead too long for the paramedics to do any resuscitation. Then the police impounded his computer. Then we had to look as they took his body away down the stairs and out of the house.

There would have to be a post-mortem.

And there was the burial to arrange.

Aileen and I were poleaxed with grief and questions.

We had not said goodbye.

In the immediate aftermath we talked and wept at the opportunities we had missed.

The drugs that were found on him included Gabapentin.

As we went over the drugs, I remembered that I had made some attempts to get help.

Once when I was terrified, I talked to my GP Dr Baines. He said to bring Reuben to see him. His policy was to give a very small dose of anti-depressants which meant he would not harm himself. I did not persuade Reuben to visit Baines.

In New Brighton, where Aileen lived, Reuben went to see a local doctor. The last time Reuben went to the surgery the local doctor was not there. He saw another doctor who gave him two week's supply of drugs – more than enough for him to take too much.

Reuben prided himself, as addicts all too often do, on his knowledge. The drugs did not control him because he could control the drugs.

DOI: 10.4324/9781003272670-5

We searched for a suicide note. He loved words and he would have written an angry, sad, devastating note. There was none. He had not meant to die. Aileen and Nick have both pointed out to me that one reason I mention suicide is that my mother committed suicide – and Reuben who loved her was very upset by that.

Child suicide makes guilt and suffering even harder. Linda Hurcombe (2007) gives a candid account of her daughter Caitlin's sudden spiral into mental health distress. On April 6, 1987 Hurcombe found her daughter dead.

> If asked to describe most commonly felt experiences in a thing a child bereaved parents will likely say I feel so alone, so isolated with grief or Nobody understands what I'm going through not my own family, not the counsellors, not the police.

Britain loves animals and Hurcombe gives an example of the idiotic consequences. She met a friend in a post office who begged her to give her a hug because she had been through a similar loss.

Her son? Her daughter?

No, her horse. She had had to have her favourite horse put down. Hurcombe points out she does not mean to belittle the pain of having a poodle or cat or elephant put down, but points out the comparison is stupid and hurtful.

After Reuben died, I had the idea that it would help Aileen to have a dog. We went to find a puppy someone could not care for as he or she had a job. Bella, a Jack Russell, became – and still is – Aileen's devoted dog. Aileen sometimes says she is better at looking after her dog than she was at looking after Reuben. She waves me away when I say she is being too harsh on herself.

"We are broken into pieces and some of those pieces are missing. How will all the people I cherish be able to deal with the person I have become?", Hurcombe (2004) asked.

A suicide note can tell truths parents did not know. Changes in our perception of the person's identity after death can be troubling. Simon Shimshon Rubin, an Israeli professor, describes it as a kind of relational trauma – that is as destructive as other forms of trauma.

Darian Leader, the psychoanalyst, argues that on an unconscious level, we start to engage with the fact that maybe there was something about the person we have lost, that we didn't know, and there was always something perhaps strange and unknown about them.

> Very often you find that, in later phases of mourning, someone will look at a photograph or a memento and it will seem strange to them; it's like, who is that? It's a very, very odd experience. It can happen in a dream, that someone you loved can somehow seem totally alien to you, totally strange; you know them, but who are they? What do they want? When we love someone, we're always imposing our own projections onto them. In the work of mourning, there's a process whereby those projections are questioned or challenged or stripped away, and we're confronted with the

tension between our projections and the reality of that person, which can be a very disturbing experience.

(Leader, 2009)

For us the only blessing was that he would not have suffered.

As Reuben's death had been sudden there had to be an inquest. We got out of the taxi and walked up the grand municipal staircase leading to the Coroner's court in Hamilton Square. We waited for our turn outside. Another family was also waiting and a reporter from the local paper *The Liverpool Echo*, who wrote a respectful tribute.

We filed into the court. Coroner is possibly the most ancient office in the land. Death is inexplicable and yet has to be explained, to the authorities at least.

Reuben's brother Nick had a friend from his days at Cambridge, Sarah Lefever, who had become a barrister and kindly agreed to represent us. She was helpful as the pathologist tried to argue Reuben had committed suicide. He had left no note. He had plans for the next day.

The Coroner at one point described Reuben as unemployed. I got up angrily and pointed out he was a freelance editor. I can't remember if I then gave him a list of the some of the books he had edited and published. The Coroner withdrew the remark.

In the end the verdict was death by misadventure. It mattered to us. Desperately. Verdicts do not matter to the dead, but they do to the living. The official verdict was he had not intended to die. After my mother committed suicide, Reuben would never have put us through the ordeal of killing himself.

I shudder even now when I pass through Hamilton Square.

Some families face a brutal aftermath. Kevin Wells and his wife had to handle the fact that when a child is murdered, the family are the first suspects. As this book is a tribute it is important to remember that Reuben worked with Kevin on the editing of *Goodbye Dearest Holly*. Kevin wrote:

"Our computer is seized and taken away. Routine, we're told."

Trudie, the policewoman assigned to the family, then tells them that "as a matter of procedure at some stage a team will visit our house to complete a detailed search. This seems completely inappropriate." The family feel that judging them is the wrong priority. That evening the family try to get some sleep but the bell rings. "I go downstairs, open the door and see a posse of police officers. To add to the weird effect, they are all dressed in black" (Wells, 2001).

Kevin asks if they could come at a better time. The answer is "No."

Nicola and I sit in the living room and have a grand stand view of every conceivable item being searched. From the loft to the downstairs toilet. Things are picked up, opened and examined. Books are feathered through, CDs, tape cassettes and drawers opened. Every piece of furniture is lifted off the ground with military precision. The police lift up the sofa on which Kevin and Nicola have been sitting.

(Wells, 2001)

The floor beneath is wooden and Kevin wonders what they imagine might be underneath. Being treated like suspects makes them "angry at the intrusion."

Finally, the police asked them to complete a list of family and friends who might be involved in the disappearance of Holly and Jessica.

The police's behaviour is based on the fact that all too often families are guilty when children disappear. But Kevin and Nicola are left angry. Kevin found himself crying and hit his head. He felt the need to do something and went on a search of local villages. Then they heard a newsflash that the girls had been seen. Their euphoria did not last long. Why had the police not told them? They were frightened and confused; typical reactions bereaved parents go through.

Aileen believes:

> I think we all need to talk more about shock. I was in shock for some years after Reuben's death and didn't know it until it started to wear off. When I went on a Compassionate Friends retreat a few months after Reuben died, the other parents said it did not hit them totally the first year. I didn't believe them – but they were right. Your head knows, and the rest of you is way, way behind.
>
> Something else seldom mentioned is the dark side of grief. Grief is not pretty. It's messy and murky. I was taken aback when I visited the US after Reuben's death by how deeply I envied my siblings their intact families. It really took me by surprise, and I think it would be wise to talk about it more. Talking about things like that is very hard to do honestly and there has to be a degree of trust, which can be hard to come by. These are not feelings people necessarily want to acknowledge, or even know about.

6 Reuben as a writer

In his moving poem *An Arundel Tomb* Philip Larkin looked at the tombs and added that "what will survive of us is love" (1988). He was a fine writer but ignored the endless bits and pieces the dead leave behind – letters, bank statements, wage slips and much else. Reuben was a writer and I have trawled through his published and unpublished material. His writings reveal despair and confusion which make them hard to read. What follows is a small selection of his work, and I hope it reaches a wide audience.

In July 2001 he wrote "Relativity and the single male" which he sent to the *Absinthe Literary Review*.

> No one gets over anything, we can't unless we kid ourselves. She says and then swigs back her absinthe not noticing it is still aflame. I fear for her life and then think simply fuck it. It's her problem. Won't shut up anyway. Incinerated lungs and sudden death would mean at least that I could go piss.
>
> It's bullshit. She slurs apparently untroubled by the napalm in her throat. Fucking category mistake. Think Eisen,. . . no Eis no not that Russian motherfucker, the kike. It's a curve right? Or a full blown fucking circle, no straight line.
>
> Green smoke shoots from her lungs and a stench of scorching flesh wafts by.

Then comes the self hate I dread to find. Is it fiction or what he really felt? He says "You should know exactly what I mean." She says "You're obviously a cripple. What was it, mummy didn't love you? Fat and friendless as a boy?"

And then the crunch, "From the look of things – her eyes touch square on mine, lit by the inner backdraft to a deep Satanic glare 'I'd say you've always failed.'"

Is that what he felt about himself?

Reuben was also at work on a novel *Theo's Ruins*. Its main character was a troubled psychoanalyst. Reuben also described a character based on himself who went to the States and lived in a commune. He described many experiences of taking drugs there and a number of sexual experiences.

As I have said, Reuben worked for Sonia Land. Her assistant Sam Boyce liked *Theo's Ruins*. But felt it was too long and was concerned by the narrative voice. She wanted him to re-work the book and make it move faster.

DOI: 10.4324/9781003272670-6

We thought the book was excellent. We tried to get it published. We sent it to Max Porter at Granta, but they did not take it. Reuben had been on an Arvon course where he was taught by Andrew O'Hagan.

O'Hagan believed Reuben would be one of the writers of his generation. We met him at the Athenaeum, a chilly club. He was sad at our loss – he came dressed in black. He was sure he could get the book published but that turned out not to be the case. So, for now the book remains unpublished. Reuben's second novel is also unpublished.

The Shifting Sands

> *The Shifting Sands* is the landscape of Ben Carmi's soul, a world re-ordered in the footsteps of his mixed nomadic family. Part American, part Israeli, raised in the UK, part Catholic, part Jewish, with these many parts never quite combining to become a single whole,

Reuben wrote. It was a trilogy.

> The first novella *Coast Roads of the 1980s* opens with Ben alone travelling to the unspecified place known only as the City on a Eurostar network which has mysteriously expanded to include Lisbon. At the ag of thirty he is returning from the wedding of a college friend, an event which has filled him with despair. Unhappily besotted with his best friend Justine, now dating his shadow Dan Kahane, he is adrift in hack work, incipient alcoholism and a profound sense of failure. More than his depression, though, the wedding has stirred up memories of the one such ceremony he had previously attended as a child in Cape Cod, and the suicide he had witnessed there.
>
> Aboard the train he finds a copy of *The Boston Globe* and learns as he drinks off his hangover that the hotel which hosted said wedding was demolished that very past weekend – a place which had haunted him for twenty years is no more. As the train tunnels down into the earth he is swept off into a drunken reverie and the confusions of his childhood.

After a brief note Reuben detailed the confusion. At the wedding he and his brother saw "their mother Ruth snorting cocaine with her siblings. This is not what one would call a nuclear family – drugs aside, Ruth is a lesbian now and the boys' absentee Jewish father an itinerant philanderer."

The one book Reuben did get published was not a novel, but a history of reality TV.

Shooting Reality

The book described the history of cinema and TV from the time that the French Assemblée Générale acquired patents to daguerreotypes. The authors interviewed Charles Parsons who created the show *Survivor* which was then bought by Endemol who changed it into *Big Brother*.

Subjecting their contestants to seclusion from the outside world, *Shooting Reality* explored the emergence of the form, its relation to documentary and its significance in a globalised TV industry. It drew parallels between some of the methods employed to control contestants and techniques of incarceration and psychological interrogation and exposed the nefarious influence of psychologists and psychotherapists in the business of reality TV. This "ultimate form of light entertainment" is also shown to be a perfect propaganda vehicle for an anti-political culture in which, in the absence of grand narratives, the personal focus, the detritus of selfhood, has come to be seen as the only story worth telling.

Reuben had access because I knew Dan Chambers and, for a while, I was the body language expert on the show. I was dropped because I stood on my head in the Big Brother chair. Making fun was not allowed.

One of Reuben's editorial triumphs was to get a graphic novel called *100 Months* (2010) into print. It is a savage and brilliant meditation on death by John Hickleton who ironically died before the book was published.

I dedicated the new edition of my first book to Reuben. None of that could hide the truth that Reuben left far too little behind.

Reuben was also well into another novel called *Thrills of Light*. I hope the excerpt from *Theo's Ruins* at the end of this book gives some sense of what a brilliant writer he was — and if only he had lived to write more.

7 What children know about death

Saying goodbye and spiritualism

Saying goodbye – one father wrote, "I know that later I would have hated myself if I had not done that and seen my child. Afterwards I was really happy that she [the nurse] forced me to say a proper goodbye to my child." It is also vital for the dying child.

Most research has concentrated on infants who die through miscarriage, stillbirth, new-born death or Sudden Infant Death Syndrome (SIDS). Until recently most professionals regarded these as "non-events" or "non-deaths" as the dead were "non-persons." Academia can be heartless.

Medical literature has not studied what children see on TV much and this is an important omission. By the time they are six years' old children routinely see death in TV dramas. Television companies show *Murder She Wrote*, Poirot and many other programmes that wield the dagger at times when children are likely to see them. News bulletins frequently highlight death. So, a child who is dying has often seen death and mourning on the screen. As did children during the 1939–1945 war when the psychiatrist John Bowlby and the psychologist Mary Ainsworth developed their theory of attachment and loss. When a child is separated from his or her mother especially, he or she becomes very distraught. Bowlby's work, in particular, makes it very clear why losing a child is so traumatic.

The psychoanalyst Darian Leader stresses the uncertainty death triggers. He writes:

> on an unconscious level, we start to engage with the fact that maybe there was something about the person we have lost, that we didn't know, and there was always something perhaps strange and unknown about them. Very often you find that, in later phases of mourning, someone will look at a photograph or a memento and it will seem strange to them; it's like, who is that? It's a very, very odd experience. It can happen in a dream, that someone you loved can somehow seem totally alien to you, totally strange; you know them, but who are they? What do they want? When we love someone, we're always imposing our own projections onto them. In the work of mourning, there's a process whereby those projections are

DOI: 10.4324/9781003272670-7

questioned or challenged or stripped away, and we're confronted with the tension between our projections and the reality of that person, which can be a very disturbing experience.

(Leader, 2009)

Today the death of a very tiny, sick or deformed new-born is no longer routine. Doctors may let parents hope a child will survive and that makes them love and hope more. Sometimes, however, discussions before the birth between the paediatrician and parents lead to a decision not to perform a life-saving operation, but the parents change their minds after the child is born when the symptoms of a lifelong disability are only minimally apparent.

Parents suffer and fear as does their child. In the 1940s and 50s there were pioneering works on how children and adolescents understood their coming death (Nagy, 1948). There has been some progress since then but not enough (Bluebond-Langner, 1978; Sourkes, 1995).

Obviously the end of life is the toughest of times and many healthcare providers have little experience in talking about it. Bell et al. (2010) talked to parents after their child had died. It is a very difficult area of research and many questions remain unanswered.

What children know about death

The way children understand death can be broken down into four parts: universality (all living things die), irreversibility (once dead, dead forever), nonfunctionality (all functions of the body stop) and what causes death. Infants and toddlers usually cannot differentiate death from separation from those who care for them. It is only when they are about ten years' old that children achieve a more complete understanding of death.

When asked about the causes of death, 5–6-year-olds usually talk about non-natural causes like violence while 8–9-year-olds usually cite illness. Perhaps surprisingly 11–12-year-olds usually point to spiritual causes like it is one's time, Bates and Kearney (2015) found that a quarter of 5–6-year-old children thought dead people could no longer feel emotion and hunger. Children tend to understand that death puts an end to physical abilities – the dead cannot eat or walk – before they understand it also puts an end to more cognitive or emotional abilities. The result is that younger children sometimes wonder what it would feel like to be dead. Jay et al. (1987) found that children with cancer are less likely than healthy children to view death as some kind of justice or punishment.

Information about prognosis is often filtered from physician to parent to child, and each step may include delays. Wolfe, Klar and Grier (2000) interviewed 103 parents of children who died from cancer as well as the children's oncologists. On average, physicians recognised there was no chance of a cure 206 days before death, but parents did not grasp that until 106 days before death. Families want to know about the prognosis, and early recognition of a dire prognosis by doctors and parents is associated with early discussions about how to manage the progression of the condition and the final stages. However even experienced medical staff find it hard to accept there is no longer any chance of recovery. Then, even if parents know the reality, they do not always tell their sick child, particularly if parents disagree with the physician's opinion. Rosenberg et al. found that parents were more likely to believe that a cure was possible. How human!

When they learn what their fate will be, some children have months, even years to understand and come to terms with it, while others have very little time. Most children with cystic fibrosis now have decades to understand what their terminal illness means to them, while a child with cancer may only have hours or days until their death. Bell et al. (2010) reported that half of the initial end-of-life discussions with adolescents who died from cancer began when patients were within their last month of life. A study in Taiwan describes how children, mostly with cancer, who died in hospital were given do-not-resuscitate orders for the first time on the last day of life in 58 per cent of cases (Tang-Her et al., 2007).

When young patients are not told about their prognosis, it not only gives them less time to process the facts, but also denies them the chance to see how their parents try to cope. It also robs them of the chance to share fears and seek comfort with family and friends. It may even mean that they do not get to say goodbye to mothers, fathers, siblings, grandparents. Adolescents especially feel it is their right to know what their prognosis is, and even younger children often know or suspect that there is more information available than what they have been told. The silence of parents and hospital staff also gives unintentional clues. Impending doom can make us go quiet. The silence of the last hours of life prefigures the silence of the tomb, that undiscovered country from which no one returns. Children may hide what they know or suspect to protect their parents. Although some children do not want to know the details of their prognosis not offering to communicate with them about it generally leads to more distress. The unknown is frightening enough, but if there is less opportunity to talk about what is going to happen it makes it more difficult to understand and accept it.

Wolfe et al. (2000) found that 89 per cent of children who died from cancer suffered "a lot" or "a great deal" from at least one physical symptom in the last month of life. Treatment for pain and dyspnoea was only successful in 27 per cent and 16 per cent of cases respectively. In the face of severe pain, children may say they do not care if they die or talk of suicidal thoughts.

Paediatric delirium occurs in approximately 20–30 per cent of patients in critical care settings. The prospect of your child dying is confusing as well as painful. Parents, aware and only partly aware of the imminence of death, may find it hard to have a meaningful conversation with their child in the last hours or days of life. In Bell et al.'s (2010) sample of adolescents who died from cancer, almost 40 per cent were using an anxiolytic medication, suggesting anxiety is another major factor for children with terminal illnesses.

Older adolescents were particularly likely to be using anxiolytics, which might reflect their greater understanding, and thus greater distress. Theunissen et al. (1998) surveyed parents after their child's death from cancer and found that sadness was the most common psychological symptom experienced by dying children, and described more psychological symptoms in children older than 12 compared with younger ones. Far from offering sensitive care, healthcare staff addressed only 43 per cent of the psychological symptoms experienced by children. They managed even less well with parents as only 56 per cent of their psychological symptoms were addressed,

Your child is dying yet the doctors and nurses tiptoe round the subject which tends to leave parents ill-equipped to support their children and more at risk of psychological complications during bereavement.

Theunissen et al. (1998) reported dying children fear being alone, physical problems and medical treatment, which may reflect the fact they know that others will not be dying with them. Children may also fear being replaced – "when I'm gone they'll love my brother and sister more and they will all carry on living."

Some children worry their parents will not be able to recover emotionally – and they worry about and resent being separated from familiar objects such as their clothes and toys. Popular culture has an impact so dying children may fear monsters, ghosts or other evil or punishing figures, who may torture them in who knows what ways. Talking with children about common fears is likely to reduce distress.

Bates and Kearney also found that terminally ill patients under the age of 15 may become increasingly aware of still being alive, wanting to live life to the fullest. A parent interviewed in a study of how families are supported in hospices was surprised to find that "children wanted to live, to have the best time possible." The same study found that young people with a terminal illness want to go out and meet other children who are well. Adolescents are also interested in sex. They can fret about things that alter their body image. "Who would kiss me when I'm stuck with many tubes. I look like an octopus with metal arms?"

There is often two-way depression. How can a parent praise a child who has no bright future? How can a child deal with that?

If children and adolescents are not given information about their illness, it makes them anxious, mistrustful and feel isolated. Until recently young people were routinely kept in the dark about their terminal diagnosis. What they need to know is often obvious, achieved simply by being present, listening and asking open-ended questions to find out what children already know, believe or can understand. The age of the dying child matters. With very young children play or drawing may be easier than speech, some argue but how do you draw death?

Children, and even adolescents, generally want their parents to be involved in important decisions. Parents commonly want to communicate information to their child themselves, especially younger children, sometimes with a clinician present to help and support them, A version of the Five Wishes advanced care planning document tailored to young patients, *Voicing My Choices* (Zadeh,

Pao and Wiener, 2015), is useful and patients recommended that it was used as soon as possible. For younger patients, family-based or group-based interventions may be helpful for starting difficult conversations in a nonthreatening way. Communication about death should be renewed with each significant development in the illness and as the child matures.

One paper highlighted the need for children to be given intervention that can improve the feeling of comfort, as revealed by four participants (Hu et al., 2019). For example, a quotation from a parent:

> The same feeling whether at home or hospital, this disturbance is nauseating. She needs acupressure.

In addition to parents, some nurses also revealed the following:

> If he complains like that, for example complaining of pain do relaxation techniques distraction or whatever. . .
> When he is receiving intravenous access, he will ask to be carried by his mother. The parents are allowed to participate, holding and accompanying the child.

Four parents revealed that they were worried the child would become sicker if the treatment took too long in hospital. For instance:

> If the child was hospitalized, the child becomes sensitive, get cough and flu, does not occur when treated at home, I'm afraid she's getting a virus.

Four parents revealed that children need ongoing home care, as expressed below by one participant:

> At home, I'm sometimes confused, she usually have nausea, fever, vomit after chemotherapy, I do not know how to treat those symptoms.

Children need information tailored to their age and developmental level. One of the nurse respondents has experience with teenage children who can find their own information about the condition of the disease through the internet. According to nine nurses and four parents they expected the children not to be given information about the terminal condition of the illness. However, four nurses stated that the purpose of the nurse giving the child information about the condition is to help the child to accept their condition. As disclosed in the following statements:

> The child is afraid of his illness, . . . we cannot directly explain to the child, . . . his mother does not allow health care team to explain about his illness in front of her son. So, if we want to explain the illness to the son is through his parents.

Three nurses and five parents revealed that the information given to parents needs to be detailed, clear and accurate. It should also be appropriate to the level of education and knowledge. Below are some sample quotations from nurses:

> A little information or the deterioration of the patient's condition, . . . a change in patient's condition is always given information to the family, sometimes family does not accept the child's condition, but if we have been slowly giving the information, the family finally accepted.

Give a clear explanation that is as detailed as possible. And then the prognosis, look at the evidence, that is usually the best way to help the patient's family understand.

The most important need for the family is information. Good information, accurate information, in accordance with what clinicians describe as a pathway. They need to know about the medication or therapy.

According to four nurses, it is important to provide motivation for children and families because that helps to improve the quality of life of children with terminal illness and also their families. The children need support, entertainment and jokes and do not want to be treated like a sick child. Nurses made the following statements:

> Motivate how the quality of their life can be better, so that they accept their condition, their family too.
>
> They need a little joy. Because in terminal patients they have been hospitalized for a long time. More about their psychological, some of them assuming we are their friend not the nurse.

Below is a statement from a parent that relates to the nurses' comments.

> Ever complained when I can eat that kind of food, . . . When I recover, I want to eat all things I want, like my brother.

According to four nurses, parents' anxiety can have a negative effect on the child. Therefore, it is important to overcome the parents' anxiety so they can provide care for children with a terminal illness as is exemplified by the following respondents:

> Because of the condition of this unstable child who at any time can die so, the parents' anxiety is the highest.
>
> When parents are anxious the child will also be anxious. We must try to calm the parents first, later if for example the parents are already calm they can also calm their son as well.

Four nurses stated that children with a terminal illness need parental involvement in their care. Children need the presence of parents when they are given have an intervention as the following quotation shows:

The mother is always included when the child receiving interventions, her presence can provide tranquility for children.

Seven participants stated that families need to be given information and advice to assist them in decision-making, as well as in providing care for their children both when the children are in hospital and at home.

Sudden Infant Death Syndrome

SIDS deaths declined by 46 per cent from 1983–1996 due to successful education and advertising campaigns. This type of death makes parents struggle with guilt even more than usual. Could the death have been prevented? Family and friends often do not know how to respond and therefore withdraw, creating a "conspiracy of silence." Parents often become intensely preoccupied with thoughts and images of the dead baby. The period of time after it becomes clear a child will die allows parents to prepare and prevent unnecessary bereavement distress after the death. Experts recommend some strategies though there are no easy answers.

1. Help parents accept the reality of their loss by gently encouraging them to see, hold, and name their dead baby and to hold and then participate in memorial services.
2. Help parents retain important mementos such as photographs and locks of hair, hand and footprints, tangible reminders and "evidence" of the child's presence such as bedding and clothing.

This advice ignores dreams which Freud, of course, claimed are wish fulfilments. I am not a Freudian and I do not often remember my dreams. I have had images of Reuben in some dreams but only occasionally. I wish I had more because I would be able to see him but they don't often come or I do not remember them when I wake up.

Darian Leader (2009) suggests that

> not necessarily immediately, but sometime after the experience of loss, rather than having dreams about the person you've lost, there may be a dream about your telling someone else about that person, or about the loss, as if something has changed in your relationship with the person you've lost. This sort of dream suggests you're no longer inhabiting the same space; you could have dreams maybe for a year or two, that you're fighting with a dead person, and then you could have a dream where you're on a stage talking about them. That's very different, it means something's changed: you no longer inhabit the same space as the dead.

The unconscious seems to worry we need to guard against the dead. "Very often people have dreams where they're killing someone who's already dead," Leader argues. Again, many rituals in different cultures involve someone being buried twice; there's a first burial and then a year later, or six months later, there's another burial, which implies that now the person is finally laid to rest. And can't come back.

Leader also discusses "settling debts with the dead." The thought "I should have done more" can haunt someone for decades after a death. That's a pretty normal reaction to a loss, but sometimes this can become amplified and exaggerated and take over a whole life," he wrote. He gives a macabre example of such a debt: "if I had paid more money for the casket, it would be OK." Another example would be, if I had said to this person how much I love them before they died it would be OK, or if I had spent this money on the flowers. All these things are treated as if they could be settled in reality, if you could just turn the clock back.

So, in mourning it's very important to distinguish things that can be paid and things that can't. This can happen at an unconscious level, it can happen in therapy, it can happen without therapy. It happens in different ways for people, there's no rule.

Leader offers what he calls a "clinical vignette" (Lertzman, 2010).

> One of my patients was obsessed with the footage from 9/11 and would spend all day, every day watching again and again all the available footage of the towers. She didn't know why she was doing it, but she had to do it, as if there was something so unimaginable about the whole thing that all she could do was try to see it from every possible viewpoint. Then she remembered that when she was a child she also, for several months, spent all her time trying to represent from every possible angle, a particular scene in which there had been a savage act of violence between her parents, which she could only see from one angle. It's very interesting to see the comparison and how it was the engagement with what had happened in the towers that brought back her childhood memories. It shows that one's response to a tragic event, on a public scale, will have very different resonances for different people on a private scale.

In the past one comfort was talking to the dead or imagining you are doing so.

Let me speak to him or her

Arthur Conan Doyle, the creator of Sherlock Holmes, wrote that there is "no time in the recorded history of the world when we do not find traces of preternatural interference and a tardy recognition of them from humanity" (Conan Doyle, 1926). The dread of mortality has always inspired the dream of immortality. It is not just selfish; we want to know that the child is safe and content, and to believe that they are thinking of us just as much as we are thinking of them. Ultimately he wrote more than a dozen books on the subject. His two-volume *The History of Spiritualism* (1926) starts by claiming the movement as "the most important in the history of the world since the Christ episode," then proposes the Swedish mystic Emanuel Swedenborg and the Scottish reformer Edward Irving, as forerunners of the Victorians.

Mary Todd Lincoln, who lost three of her four children, visited mediums in Georgetown before hosting her own séances in the Red Room of the White House. She also hired the country's most famous "spirit photographer" to take a picture of her with her husband after he was assassinated. Peter Manseau's *The Apparitionists: A Tale of Phantoms, Fraud, Photography, and the Man Who Captured Lincoln's Ghost* (2017) offers a fascinating account of that photographer, William H. Mumler, who worked as a jewellery engraver in Boston before taking a self-portrait that, when developed, revealed what became known as an "extra": in his case, a young girl sitting in a chair to his right, whom he recognised as a cousin who had died a dozen years before. Mourning portraits – paintings of the recently dead – had been popular for a long time, but spirit photographs offered something more: not just remembering lost loved ones but confirmation of life after death.

Almost a third of Americans say they have communicated with someone who has died and spend more than two billion dollars a year on psychic services. Instagram, Facebook, TikTok, TV: whatever the medium, there is a medium advertised. Then there are more than 100 Spiritualist churches in the United States, more than 300 in the United Kingdom.

When I was a teenager, I had an elocution teacher who was a Spiritualist and we did a brief extract from Wilde's *The Importance of Being Earnest* (1895) for her congregation.

Mrs Croucher seemed eccentric to me, but early Spiritualism attracted some of the great scientists of the day, including the physicists Marie and Pierre Curie, the evolutionary biologist Alfred Russel Wallace and the psychologist William James, all of whom believed that modern scientific methods, far from standing in opposition to the spiritual realm, could finally prove its existence. Mark Twain and Queen Victoria both attended séances.

Popular memoirs such as *Evenings at Home in Spiritual Séance* (Houghton, 2013) and *Shadow Land; or Light from the Other Side* (d'Espérance, 2012) reinforced that interest in survival after death. The Society for Psychical Research was founded in 1885. The psychologist William James was one of its first presidents.

Agatha Christie's books often include seances. One fine one takes place in *Dumb Witness* (2018) where a dog called Bob helps Poirot solve the murders. In the end, although Poirot cannot imagine living with a dog and manages to persuade two clairvoyant sisters that he has heard from the Other Side, it was their dead spaniel that told him Bob is destined to live with them.

In one of the most publicised attempts to test the claims of Spiritualists, *Scientific American* offered $5000 to anyone who could produce evidence which would convince a committee that consisted of academics from Harvard and the Massachusetts Institute of Technology, psychic experts and Harry Houdini, the great escapologist, who knew something about illusions and developed a side-line in exposing those which hucksters were trying to pass off as real, of survival after death. Armed with electroscopes and galvanometers, the committee tested all the mediums who presented themselves for scrutiny, sometimes attending multiple séances before rendering a verdict.

Spiritualism eventually became a kind of curiosity, a Victorian fad encountered chiefly in the biographies of artists such as Elizabeth Barrett Browning, who dabbled in mesmerism, in the footnotes to the modernist poetry of T. S. Eliot and W. B. Yeats, with their invocations of astrology and sorcery, and Madame Blavatsky, in museum exhibits of the mystical paintings of Hilma af Klint and in horror films like *Ouija* (2014) and *Things Heard & Seen* (2017). Spiritualism is most often invoked only to be discredited, and cynical accounts routinely sneer at the sincerity or impugn the sanity of individual believers, unwilling or unable to imagine the appeal of a movement that dominated religious life both here and abroad for several decades.

We want answers because parents feel what has happened is unjust and are sometimes furious with healthcare professionals, their spouse, God or fate. Alternatively, these emotions may be directed inward towards themselves, resulting in lowered self-esteem, self-blame and depression. Parents also experience intense anger and jealousy towards other parents whose babies are still alive.

It is no surprise that the Web offers advice on how to get in touch with the dead. I quote this material not because I believe in it, but because it shows how much we can want the dead to give us some sign that they are still out there. So, with a pinch of salt, I quote from Souvik Ray in "13 Signs That Show The Spirit World Is Trying To Make Contact With You" (2021).

He argued that:

> Just the thought of a spirit making contact with us, is both exciting and scary. Here are just some ways the spiritual world might just be trying to say hello. We didn't simply make these up, experienced psychics who have played mediums between the living and the dead gave us a few pointers, as did people who claim they felt some kind of supernatural connection with loved ones who had recently passed away. A lot of people also believe that there are spiritual signs that death is near.

Ray warns "however, this doesn't mean this is scientific or proven facts. Choose what you want to believe." His list includes clocks that have stopped. If the time reminds you of a deceased person, perhaps the time they died, or the time you received the news of their demise, you are being visited. I have put in a few cynical asides.

You can always ask what time it is in their dimension.

Flickering and blowing out light-bulbs

Psychics believe that spirits can manipulate electricity, suggesting that flickering light-bulbs can be a sign indicating that spirits are present in your room. Some people have complained about light-bulbs blowing out despite being newly installed.

Ray adds "You might call this absolute *bakwaas*, but let me tell you, it has happened in my house where new light-bulbs have on several occasions gone out. Perhaps they were defective, my opinion on the subject remains neutral." *Or you haven't paid your electricity bill.*

Ray suggests contacting the being in your mind by asking the question, "who is this?", a face and name will come to you.

Changes in room temperature

Sudden drops in warmth despite door and windows being closed also signify the presence of a supernatural being.

It may be described as a cold chill through the body that can give us goose-bumps when we unconsciously think of the presence of spiritual beings close by.

If you detect an eerie aura, take care and check your central heating.

Sounds and music

Hearing your name being called out in your head or simply hearing noises that are inaudible to everyone else is also claimed to be a sign that loved ones from the afterlife are trying to make contact.

Sometimes random songs may play in our head and again on T.V. If we realize that this song or music has something to do with a deceased person, it could just be their spirit saying hello.

Butterflies

I especially like butterflies.

The ancient Chinese believed that butterflies were symbolic of people who had left the realm of the living owing to the transformation from cocoons to their short lifespan of fluttering in the air. If you see butterflies or related motifs after the death of a person, it is a sign that the person has moved into the spirit world.

Faces of people who lived

Many clients reported that they saw people who looked like their relatives who had passed away a long time ago. Perhaps the people didn't actually look like their relatives but their minds saw differently. I have sometimes seen Reuben in my mind or men who look like him.

Shadows out of the corner of your eye

Ray notes

it's happened to me, so I thought I would share my experience with you. I was browsing the internet one night when I subconsciously noticed a black object rise up towards the ceiling from the corner of my eye. It was like the shadow of a bird, but when I looked up and to my side, there was nothing.

I for one believe what the psychic had to say about this, but perhaps science has its own reasoning.

Touches

Ticklish and pressure type sensations can often be felt on the face and body. It could be stroking of hair, jabs on the sides and unexplained pain in the foot. Psychics suggest asking the spirit of a loved one to touch you on, say, the right side of your face, to make sure that it is them rather than some malign force.

Computers

Computers acting on their own, downloading documents, sending emails that you didn't send yourself and the names of deceased relatives appearing on the screen might also be a sign of visiting spirits. A computer engineer would however blame a virus and ask you to upgrade your software.

Dreams and visions

They might be vivid and comforting or they might be horrifying and disturbing. However, they all carry a twisted message that does not make sense and is open to interpretation. Psychics suggest keeping a notepad by your bedside because most of these dreams end with us waking up almost immediately after it is over. And as human as we are, we forget about it.

If the dreams you see of loved ones are disturbing and upsetting, Ray recommends that you turn to religion and prayer to seek solace. *He does not say what atheists should do.*

Telepathic thoughts

If you are hearing your voice in your head speaking words that are not your thoughts, you are probably hearing what a spirit is trying to tell you. It may be repeated several times for emphasis.

Scents

When Ray lived in South East Asia, he was often warned that a sudden burst of floral fragrances in unlikely places signifies the presence of a spirit. A friend would always smell a floral scent in her car even though she did not have an air purifier.

It stopped only after she opened the doors of her car and aggressively demanded the spirit to leave.

Go pester that SUV behind us may be useful to say.

Photographs

Wall and photos and table frames falling flat, becoming crooked or developing a certain form of mist or mould on the picture also signify a spiritual presence. However, this is said to happen if the picture is of a deceased person.

Photographs that are clicked with a digital camera sometimes produce images with orb like structures. Psychics believe that these are not problems with the lens or focus but spirits captured on camera. They might be trying to highlight their presence to the photographer.

Ray does not mention our four-legged friends. Dogs and other animals can see what humans can't. And toddlers are said to better sense spirits as they are more intuitive. Watching your pets and young children for odd behaviour or strange messages can reveal the presence of spirits.

A final piece of advice from the Web. Buy one of the latest Ouija boards as well as electronic devices that will detect a ghost in your larder. Often despite investing in the best equipment, there is no definite answer or explanation, which is frustrating.

It is time to return to proper psychology.

Stage theories

Psychologists like stage theories such as Piaget's theory of the development of child intelligence. Piaget and his wife observed their children from the moment they were born. He admitted that these stages were not absolute. Children varied. Grief theorists usually have not paid attention to his subtleties and read his work. The grief models propose five stages. Let us see what this academic approach delivers. According to some psychologists, grief reactions should be completed within a few weeks to a few months of a death. Done and dusted. Or to use that favourite word "closure" should take place. However, Becvar (2003) suggested that a more typical timeline begins with shock and intense grief for two weeks, followed by two months of strong grieving and then a slow recovery that takes about two years. Premature closure again. Murphy et al. (2003) found that parents reported thinking of the death of their child daily three and four years after it happened. McClowry et al. (1995) found that parents whose child died of cancer still experienced pain and a sense of loss 7–9 years after the death.

Darian Leader complained that, when seeking bereavement counselling, some people often feel absolutely enraged that they're being put into a kind of box – now you're in this stage, and then you'll move to this one and then you'll move to this one. Mourning doesn't have such neat stages. It's a very complicated thing, it takes a long time and it can also never happen. The nub of the question is, are the important moments in a mourning process conscious or not? And crucially most of the time we don't mourn. I went back to an essay

Freud wrote about mourning and for the first time, it really registered: he talks about revolt in the human mind against mourning. Why? Because mourning is so painful and it's easier in a sense to deny a loss than to try to engage with it. Which is an amazing thing: it means that even though we all lose relatives, family, people who are important to us, maybe most of the time, mourning doesn't take place.

Reuben was a man when he died but we need to consider an infant death.

When does a person begin? At conception according to Catholic doctrine. Psychologists have a more nuanced answer because of work on when a baby becomes a person.

When do we acquire person-hood?

One thousand and thirty-seven children from Dunedin in New Zealand have been studied for decades by researchers who have often interviewed not just the subjects but also their family and friends. In 2020, Jay Belsky, Avshalom Caspi, Terrie E. Moffitt and Richie Poulton summarised the results in *The Origins of You: How Childhood Shapes Later Life*. They suggest each child has his or her own particular set of traits and dynamics.

The Dunedin researchers used their results to identify five general types of children. Forty per cent of the kids were deemed "well-adjusted," with the usual mixture of child personality traits. Another quarter were found to be "confident" – more than usually comfortable with strangers and new situations. Fifteen per cent were "reserved," or standoffish, at first. About one in ten turned out to be "inhibited"; the same proportion were identified as "under controlled." The inhibited kids were notably shy and exceptionally slow to warm up; the under controlled ones were impulsive and bad-tempered. What the Dunedin study shows is that by the age of three children have a definite personality, so the death of a baby is the death of human being.

I will be less academic. You cannot escape what perturbs you. You cannot escape what would have been his or her birthday where your child is not there to hear Happy Birthday – and the questions which keep coming up. I asked myself some of these questions, though not all were relevant to Reuben and his death.

Some of the questions you can never shake off are:

> Didn't I check that she was safe? 'Why didn't the hospital tell me what the risks were?
> Why didn't he cry and wake us up?
> Why did I let my child out of my sight?
> Could we have taken away some of the suffering?
> Did we ever really had the close relationship we wanted?
> Could we have shown our love more when our child was alive?
> Why did I hurt my own child? Even if you did not.

Why was she the one to fall off the rocks?
Why was it my son who was killed in the crossfire?

And always:

Why did my child have to die?

The questions chase around inside our brain.

Life, fate, the universe owes us some answers. Fatuous hope as no explanations will ever come but the ifs surface all the time.

If only I had been more gentle.
If only I had listened when she wanted to tell me something.
If only I had taken more time to do things with him.
If only I had bought him that little truck/given her that pet rabbit/done any of those special things that would have let my child know how much I cared.

Aileen speaks of a hole in the family. We were four with our two sons. Now we are three.

A popular magazine lists the questions parents should but often don't know the answer to. They are:

1 What really makes your child angry?
2 Who is her best friend?
3 What is her favourite colour/number/food?
4 What is her favourite place to visit?
5 What embarrasses her the most?
6 Would she prefer a vanilla, strawberry or chocolate milkshake?
7 What is her biggest fear?
8 What does she struggle most with at school?
9 What is her favourite animal?
10 What is her favourite family vacation?
11 What would she like to change about her appearance?
12 What is her biggest complaint about the family?
13 Does she want to be like/different from you?
14 When was the last time she was really angry?
15 What is her favourite song/radio station?
16 If you could buy her anything in the world, what would be her first choice?
17 What is her proudest accomplishment?
18 What has been the biggest disappointment in her life?
19 What is her favourite book/game?
20 Which chores does she like/dislike the most?

21   Does she feel too small/too big for her age?
22   What gift does she cherish the most?
23   Who has influenced her life the most (outside the family)?
24   Who is her favourite teacher? Why?
25   What makes her feel sad?
26   What's her favourite joke or riddle?
27   What careers are she interested in learning more about?
28   What is her favourite movie/TV show?
29   What's something she doesn't believe she can do?
30   Rank her classes from most (1) to least (14) favourite: art, music, PE, library, Spanish, science, reading, maths, health, computer, dance, writing, social studies, spelling, etc.

Interesting questions and they highlight how parents often know so little about their children.

What makes you think, shudder and weep is your own negligence. We failed, for example, to ask obvious questions about a place Reuben often visited.

The Chislehurst Caves are a labyrinth of man-made tunnels that go 30 metres below the homes and woodlands above. They were first opened in 1900 and guides describe the history of smuggling and murder there. The caves were used for munitions storage initially and then as a venue for music concerts/festivals. Reuben and his friends went there to use drugs. We had no idea. We never asked why they went there. Reuben would bring his friends home and we asked nothing.

The murder of one child is harrowing enough but numbers matter and there is even worse. In the 1950s, 1960s and 1970s the caves were used as a venue.

8 School killings

Stalin, who was not known for his empathy, wrote that the death of one person is a tragedy but the death of thousands was a statistic. The death of children has become terrifyingly common in the US. CNN research identified 288 school shootings there between January 2009 and May 2018. By comparison, Canada and France each had two, Germany had one and Japan, Italy and the UK had none. So, the US had 57 times more school shootings in that period than all the other G7 countries combined.

Animals in the wild do sometimes kill their young but usually that is because they are starving. Human beings seem not to need such excuses. The details of school killings – mainly but not only in the US – are often vicious. They reveal much about the personality of the killer – and how survivors are affected. In a number of cases the police response was woeful and they let many children die. It would be kind to think that the events are so unnatural the police do not know how to cope. Often, however, the evidence suggests fear and funk.

In 1764 on July 26, four Lenape American Indians entered the schoolhouse near Greencastle, Pennsylvania, and killed schoolmaster Enoch Brown, and nine or ten children (reports vary). Only two children survived.

Almost a century later on November 2, 1853, in Louisville, Kentucky, a student, Matthew Ward, bought a self-cocking pistol in the morning, went to school and killed his teacher Mr Butler for punishing his brother harshly. Even though he shot Butler point blank in front of his classmates, he was acquitted.

On April 30, 1866, an editorial in the *New York Times* argued against students carrying pistols as follows:

A boy of 12 has his pantaloons made with a pistol pocket; and this at a boarding-school filled with boys, who, we suppose, do or wish to do the same thing. We would advise parents to look into it, and learn whether shooting is to be a part of the scholastic course which may be practiced on their boys; or else we advise them to see that their own boys are properly armed with the most approved and deadly-pistol, and that there may be an equal chance at least of their shooting as of being shot.

DOI: 10.4324/9781003272670-8

Predicting violent behaviour

My friend the late Dr James MacKeith was a psychiatrist who worked at Brixton Prison and Broadmoor. Inmates at the latter were usually detained at Her Majesty's Pleasure. Psychiatrists had to decide when someone was safe to release. This proved both then and now, to be very difficult, sometimes because patients are devious and sometimes because patients do not realise what triggers their obsessions. One of MacKeith's colleagues released patients too easily and a number killed again. One was Graham Young, the so-called teenage poisoner (MacKeith, 1992, personal communication). The history of those who perpetrate school violence clearly exemplifies the problems of prediction.

Dunblane

In March 1996 16 children and a teacher died at Dunblane in Scotland. The killer, Thomas Hamilton, then committed suicide. One of the pupils at the school was Andy Murray. Years later he revealed how he knew killer Thomas Hamilton as a child. He was sometimes driven by him to the kids club that Hamilton ran.

For over 20 years Andy Murray stayed silent. Then he agreed to take part in a film. However, he could not speak face-to-face about the painful experiences in the film – instead he left a voicemail for the director. He told film-maker Olivia Cappuccini:

> You asked me a while ago why tennis was important to me. Obviously, I had the thing that happened at Dunblane. . . .
>
> I am sure for all the kids there it would be difficult for different reasons. The fact we knew the guy, we went to his kids club, he had been in our car, we had driven and dropped him off at train stations and things. Within 12 months of that happening, our parents got divorced.
>
> It was a difficult time. To see that and not quite understand what is going on. Then six to 12 months after that, my brother also moved away from home. He went away to train to play tennis in Cambridge.
>
> We obviously used to do everything together. When he moved away that was also quite hard for me. Around that time and after that, for a year or so, I had lots of anxiety but that came out when I was playing tennis. When I was competing, I would get really bad breathing problems.

Frankl stressed the need for individuals to find an activity to cope with the pain of grieving. To some psychiatrists his ideas seemed ridiculous. For example, he apparently told a patient who was dying of cancer to spend time studying East Africa. Andy Murray said,

> My feeling towards tennis is that it's an escape for me in some ways. Because all of these things are stuff that I have bottled up. I don't know because we don't talk about these things.

The way that I am, on the tennis court, I show some positive things about my personality, and I also show the bad things and things I really hate. Tennis allows me to be that child, that has all of these questions and that's why tennis is important to me.

At the beginning, I was like: "Well, it is. It's important to me. I know I am very fortunate I get to play, and very lucky that this is what I get to do for my living. It's important for me for other reasons. And I don't want to talk to you about it. Maybe I will tell you later on. I don't want to discuss it."

After Dunblane, some bereaved parents campaigned for a change in the law to make private handguns virtually impossible to obtain in most of the UK. It has worked. Gun deaths are now very rare – in 2020, there were just 30 homicides using a gun in England and Wales.

Eight days after the shooting, the then-ruling Conservative Party asked senior judge Lord Cullen to carry out a public inquiry. He recommended stricter limitations, but not an outright ban, on handguns.

The UK's gun culture has never been as politically powerful as that in the US. Nevertheless, a campaigner, Gill Marshall-Andrews, said: "We were told by the shooting fraternity that there was no way we were going to get a ban on handguns because pistol shooting was the fastest-growing sport in the country at the time."

She said that the Gun Control Network began to get death threats and hoax bombs were sent to their mailing address. They also fell victim to a sort of pre-digital trolling and began to receive sacks and sacks of junk mail. In November 1997 Britain finally enacted a full ban on private ownership of handguns.

Dunblane was not a one-off. School killings occur all over the world. Usually, the gunman works alone but in the event that led to the most deaths, the killers were military.

Beslan, Russia 2004

The attack on the school took place in Beslan on September 1, the traditional start of the Russian school year, referred to as First Bell or Knowledge Day. Because of that, the number of people in the schools was much higher than normal. Early in the morning, several dozen heavily armed Islamic nationalist guerrillas left a forest near the village of Psedakh in the neighbouring republic of Ingushetia, east of North Ossetia and west of war-torn Chechnya. They wore green military camouflage and black balaclava masks, and some were also wearing explosive belts and what sounds comical "explosive underwear." Let's call them knickers that go bang.

At 09:11 the terrorists arrived in a GAZelle police van and a GAZ-66 military truck. Some at the school mistook them for Russian special forces practising a security drill. The attackers soon began shooting in the air and forcing everyone from the school grounds into the building. Some 50 people managed to flee and alert the authorities.

The attackers took approximately 1100 hostages, herded them into the school's gym and confiscated their mobile phones. When the father of one of the hostages, Ruslan Betrozov, stood up to calm people and repeat the school rules in the local language of Ossetic, a gunman approached him, asked Betrozov if he had finished, and then shot him in the head. Another father Vadim Bolloyev, who also refused to kneel, was shot too. Their bodies left a trail of blood.

Russian police and security forces surrounded the school.

The attackers mined the gym and the rest of the building with explosive devices and surrounded it with tripwires. They also threatened to kill 50 hostages for every one of their own members killed by the police, and to kill 20 hostages for every gunman injured.

The lack of food and water took a toll on the children, many of whom were forced to stand in the hot, crowded gym. Many took their clothes off because it was so hot, others fainted and parents feared that these children would die. Some hostages drank their own urine.

At about 15:30, the attackers detonated two grenades setting a police car on fire and injuring one officer, but Russian forces did not return fire. As the day and night wore on, the combination of stress and sleep deprivation – and possibly drug withdrawal – made the hostage-takers increasingly hysterical and unpredictable. The crying of the children irritated them, and often crying children and their mothers were threatened that they would be shot if they did not stop it.

Police Lieutenant Colonel Elbrus Nogayev said, "I heard a command saying, 'Stop shooting! Stop shooting!' while other troops' radios said, 'Attack!'" His wife and child died. As the fighting began, an oil-company president and negotiator Mikhail Gutseriyev (an ethnic Ingush) phoned the hostage-takers and heard, "You tricked us!" Five hours later, Gutseriyev spoke to the terrorists for the last time during which conversation a terrorist said, "The blame is yours and the Kremlin's."

A chaotic battle broke out as the special forces fought to enter the school.

By 15:00 Russian troops had claimed control of most of the school, but firefighters were not prepared to battle the blaze that raged in the gym.

The question of why the emergency services are sometimes ineffective needs to be asked.

Many of the injured died before patients were sent to better-equipped facilities in Vladikavkaz, as the only hospital in Beslan was not equipped to cope with the casualties. There was an inadequate supply of hospital beds, medication and neurosurgery equipment. Relatives were not allowed to visit hospitals where the wounded were treated a sign of Soviet-style control perhaps – and doctors were not allowed to use their mobile phones.

Many survivors remained severely traumatised and at least one female former hostage committed suicide shortly after identifying the body of her child.

President Putin made only a hurried trip to Beslan hospital. He was later criticised for not meeting the families of victims. After returning to Moscow, he ordered a two-day period of national mourning on 6 and 7 September. In his televised speech, Putin said: "We showed ourselves to be weak. And the weak get beaten."

A spokesman for Chechen independence stated: "Such a bigger blow could not be dealt upon us . . . People around the world will think that Chechens are monsters if they could attack children."

The Washington Post stated that the death toll was 334, excluding terrorists. The death toll included 186 children. In the wake of the killings, Putin tightened gun laws, which amazingly the US has not done despite many school killings.

Sandy Hook 2012

Twenty-year-old Adam Lanza killed 27 people and himself. He first killed his mother at their home before taking her guns and driving to his former elementary school in Newtown, Connecticut. He killed 20 first-grade children aged 6 and 7, along with 6 adults, including 4 teachers, the principal and the school psychologist. Two other people were injured. Lanza then killed himself as police got to the school.

Within hours of the shooting, Jones was telling his audience that it was staged as a pretext for confiscating guns. Within days, he began to suggest that grieving parents were actors. It was all faked. There has been a long legal case related to this allegation. A Connecticut jury ordered Infowars founder Alex Jones to pay $965 million in damages to the families of eight victims of the shooting for the suffering caused by years of lies that the massacre was a hoax.

William Aldenberg, then an FBI agent, went to the scene of the shooting on December 14, 2012. He, too, became a target of conspiracy theories. Chris Mattei, the lawyer for the families, asked Aldenberg if what he saw in the school that day was fake. "No, no. No, sir," he responded. Mattei asked if there were any actors there. "No," Aldenberg said, overcome with emotion. "It's awful, awful."

The families testified that the lies spread by Jones led to harassment and threats by conspiracy theorists who have accused them of faking their own children's deaths. They described feeling unsafe in their homes and hypervigilant in public. Some of the families moved away from Newtown.

During his testimony, Jones was largely unrepentant. When Mattei told Jones to show more respect for the relatives in the courtroom, Jones lashed out. "Is this a struggle session? Are we in China? I've already said I'm sorry hundreds of times, and I'm done saying I'm sorry."

"The truth matters," said Erica Lafferty, the daughter of Sandy Hook, Elementary Principal of Dawn Lafferty Hochsprung, who was killed at the school. "Those who profit off other people's pain and trauma will pay for what they've done." Jones was ordered to pay $965 million for Sandy Hook.

"It is one thing to lose a child," said Francine Wheeler whose son was killed. "It's quite another thing when people take everything about your boy who is gone, and your surviving child, and your husband, and everything you ever did in your life on the internet and harass you."

Jones supports Donald Trump, who has returned the praise. "Your reputation is amazing," Trump told Jones in late 2015, "I won't let you down." Jones' all too many fans also circulated a photo of a choir performance by children who had survived the shooting, to suggest that no children had been killed at the school.

Parkland 2018

The shooting took place on the afternoon of February 14, 2018, at Marjory Stoneman Douglas High School. Nikolas Cruz was walking round the school carrying a rifle case and a backpack. He was recognised as an ex-pupil by a staff member who radioed a colleague that he was walking "purposefully" toward Building 12.

Cruz was armed with an AR-15 style semi-automatic rifle and a large number of magazines. He began firing indiscriminately at students and teachers, killing 9 pupils and wounding 13 others. Two of the dead were students in Ivy Schamis' Holocaust History class; Schamis was teaching a lesson on combating hate when Cruz fired shots into her classroom. According to Schamis, Cruz was unaware he was shooting into a class on the Holocaust, even though he had drawn swastikas on the ammunition magazines that he left at the school.

After he stopped shooting (possibly because his rifle jammed), Cruz dropped his rifle and left by blending in with fleeing students. He then walked to a fast-food restaurant, stopping at a mall to get a soda on the way, and lingered before leaving on foot at 15:01. At about 15:40, police stopped Cruz two miles from the restaurant and arrested him.

The shooting lasted for about six minutes in total. While Special Weapons and Tactics (SWAT) paramedics were inside the building, additional paramedics from the local Fire-Rescue Department repeatedly asked for permission to enter the building. These requests were turned down by Broward Sheriff's Office, even after the suspect had been arrested.

The last victim to remain hospitalised, 15-year-old Anthony Borges, was discharged on April 4. Dubbed "the real Iron Man," Borges was shot five times after he used his body to barricade the door of a classroom in which there were 20 students. Borges issued a statement that criticised the actions of Broward Sheriff's deputies, Sheriff Scott Israel and School Superintendent Robert Runcie. His family filed notice of its intent to sue the school district for personal injury to cover costs related to Borges' recovery.

Survivors of the shooting, teachers and students alike, have struggled with survivor's guilt and other symptoms of Post-Traumatic Stress Disorder (PTSD). There have been two suicides as a result of the shooting. On March 17, 2019, 13 months after the shooting, 19-year-old Sydney Aiello, committed suicide after struggling to attend college. She was terrified of being in a classroom and also had been treated for survivor's guilt and PTSD. Less than a week later, a 16-year-old boy who had survived the shooting killed himself.

Nikolas Jacob Cruz was in serious trouble and many agencies knew that long before his shooting spree. Both his adoptive parents died, leaving him orphaned three months before his rampage.

Cruz was transferred between schools six times in an effort to deal with his behavioural problems. There were reports that he made threats against other students. He returned to Stoneman Douglas High School two years after his last expulsion but was expelled again n 2017. The school administration had circulated an email to teachers, warning that Cruz had made threats against other students. The school banned him from wearing a backpack on campus.

Psychiatrists recommended his involuntary admission to a residential treatment facility in 2013; they reported he had depression, autism and attention deficit hyperactivity disorder. However, they concluded he was "at low risk of harming himself or others." He had not received treatment in the year leading up to the shooting.

Broward County Sheriff Scott Israel described Cruz's online profiles and accounts as "very, very disturbing." They had pictures and posts of him with a variety of weapons, including long knives, a shotgun, a pistol and a BB gun. Predictably he held "extremist" views and his social media accounts had anti-black and anti-Muslim slurs. YouTube comments linked to him include "I wanna die Fighting [sic] killing [sic] shit ton of people." On September 24, 2017, a person with the username "nikolas cruz" posted a comment to a YouTube video that read, "Im [sic] going to be a professional school shooter.!" The person who uploaded the video to YouTube reported the comment to the FBI. According to FBI agent Robert Lasky, the agency conducted database reviews but was unable to track down the individual who made the threatening comment.

Sheriff Scott Israel said that his office had received 23 calls about Cruz during the previous decade, but this figure is in dispute. CNN obtained a sheriff's office log, which showed that from 2008 to 2017, at least 45 calls were made in reference to Cruz, his brother or the family home. One warned on November 30, 2017 that he might be a "school shooter in the making."

On January 5, 2018, less than two months before the shooting, the FBI received a tip on its Public Access Line from a person who was close to Cruz. On February 16, two days after the shooting, the agency released a statement that said: "The caller provided information about Cruz's gun ownership, desire to kill people, erratic behaviour, and disturbing social media posts, as well as the potential of him conducting a school shooting." After conducting an investigation, the FBI said the tip line did not follow protocol when the information was not forwarded to the Miami Field Office, which should have investigated the tip but did not.

The lack of response by Israel and other members of the Broward County Sheriff's Office to the many warnings about Cruz has been the subject of scrutiny. Scot Peterson, who was armed, on-site and in uniform as a Broward Sheriff's Office deputy, was accused of remaining outside Building 12 during the shooting. Eight days after the attack, he was suspended without pay by Sheriff Israel, and retired. Sheriff Israel said, "Scot Peterson was absolutely on campus for this entire event," and that he should have "gone in, addressed the killer, [and] killed the killer."

In June 2019, Peterson was arrested and then bonded out for the crime of failing to protect the students during the shooting.

The Miami Herald transcribed radio dispatches that Peterson made during the shooting, "At 2:27, at Building 12, he radioed, 'Stay at least 500 feet away at this point.' At an unspecified time, Peterson ordered: 'Do not approach the 12 or 1300 building, stay at least 500 feet away.'"

Unnamed sources told CNN that Coral Springs police arrived at the scene and saw three Broward deputies behind their vehicles with pistols drawn. Broward Sheriff's Office Captain Jan Jordan ordered deputies to form a perimeter instead of immediately confronting the shooter as their training recommended. Jordan was widely criticised for her actions, and she resigned, citing personal reasons, nine months after the shooting.

President Trump criticised the officers who failed to enter the building during the shooting. On February 26, 2018, he said that he would have entered "even if I didn't have a weapon, and I think most of the people in this room would have done that, too." His statement was mocked by some late night show hosts. Hero Trump had dodged the military draft.

In 2022 a Florida jury returned a verdict of life without parole for Nikolas Cruz. Three jurors voted to spare his life because there was mitigating evidence of mental illness.

Columbine 1999

In 1996, 15-year-old Eric Harris created a website on America Online and began a blog. In early 1997, the blog's postings began to show the first signs of Harris's anger. It offered instructions on how to make explosives. The site got few visitors and caused no concern until August 1997. Then Harris detailed his murderous fantasies with "All I want to do is kill and injure as many of you as I can, especially a few people. Like Brooks Brown."

After that Brown's parents contacted the Jefferson County Sheriff's Office, an investigator asked for a search warrant for the Harris household, but it was never submitted to a judge.

On January 30, 1998, Harris and his friend Dylan Klebold were arrested for breaking into a white van and stealing tools and computer equipment. They were sentenced to a juvenile diversion programme which included anger management. They were both released several weeks early because they seemed to be responding well and were put on probation.

Shortly afterwards Harris began to write his thoughts down in a journal. He typed out one plan of attack after which he would escape to a foreign country or hijack an aircraft at Denver International Airport and crash it into New York City.

Klebold had been keeping a personal journal since March 1997, and also imagined going on a killing spree. He too described his personal problems as well as what he would wear and use during the attack.

Harris described his desire to rape and torture women. He also expressed interest in cannibalism and stated that he would like to dismember a woman whom he could have sex with.

In their schoolwork both boys gloried in themes of violence in their creative writing projects. In December 1997, Harris wrote a paper titled "Guns in School," and a poem from the perspective of a bullet. Klebold wrote a short story about a man killing students which worried his teacher so much that she alerted his parents.

Harris also wrote a paper on the Nazis, while Klebold wrote one on Charles Manson, leader of the San Francisco cult that carried out several murders. Their most famous victim was actress Sharon Tate, wife of film director Roman Polanski, who was killed in her Los Angeles home along with three guests.

Nearly a year before the massacre, Klebold wrote a message in Harris's 1998 yearbook: "killing enemies, blowing up stuff, killing cops!! My wrath for January's incident will be godlike. Not to mention our revenge in the commons." The commons was slang for the school cafeteria.

A few days before the massacre, Harris left a micro cassette labelled "Nixon" on the kitchen table. It boasted: "People will die because of me" and "It will be a day that will be remembered forever."

Harris and Klebold managed to buy a veritable armoury. On November 22, 1998, their friend Robyn Anderson bought a carbine rifle and two shotguns for them as they were too young to legally buy the guns themselves. After the attack, she told investigators that she had thought the pair wanted the items for target shooting, and that she had no prior knowledge of their plans.

The sheer scale of the boys' armoury is astonishing. Harris and Klebold built 99 bombs which included pipe bombs, carbon dioxide cartridges filled with gunpowder, Molotov cocktails and propane tanks converted into bombs. The propane bombs were used in the cafeteria, and in their cars as a diversion. During the massacre, they carried match strikers taped to their forearms for easy ignition of the pipe bombs and carbon dioxide bombs.

It seems very strange that no one noticed the risk they posed, or asked how they got the money.

The most recent killing – Uvalde 2022

Many of the details in what follows come from the *Texas House Committee Report* (2022) on the tragedy at Uvalde. In November 2021 and February 2022, Salvador Ramos bought rifle slings, a military carrier vest and a snap-on trigger system – and 60 rounds of ammunition. He posted his plans for a mass shooting in the course of several interactions on social media. He spoke of doing something in May that would make him famous and put him "all over the news."

As soon as he turned 18, on May 16, 2022 Ramos bought a Daniel Defence AR-15-style rifle and 1740 rounds of ammunition. In the next few days, he bought a Smith & Wesson AR-15-style rifle and an additional 375 rounds of ammunition. He spent at least $4896 on weapons, ammunition and accessories.

The day of the shooting started dramatically. Between 11:06 and 11:20 Ramos sent text messages to an online friend in Germany moaning he was annoyed with his grandmother and that he was about to "do something to her [right now]."

Then he told his friend: "I just shot my grandma in her head. Ima go shoot up a elementary school rn [right now]." He then stole his grandmother's truck and drove to Robb Elementary School where he fired three rounds at two men near a funeral home and then fled. They were unharmed and called 911. Immediately afterwards a teacher raised the alarm. She yelled for students to get into their classrooms and called 911.

Ramos got as far as the last row of the school parking lot, firing his rifle from between vehicles. A school district police patrol vehicle entered the school parking lot and drove past Ramos without spotting him. This was the first utter failure of the police.

At 11.32 Ramos fired shots through windows into rooms on the west side of the school. The principal of the school started to implement a lockdown, including sending out an alert. Teachers began to tell their students to hide inside the classrooms. Some also closed and locked doors. A minute later Ramos entered the school through a back door on the northwest side of the school. And then walked into classroom 111.

Ramos shot at least 100 rounds in two and half minutes inside rooms 111 and 112. Children could be heard screaming. According to the *Texas House Committee Report* produced after the massacre, "the attacker fired most of his shots and likely murdered most of his innocent victims before any responder set foot in the building."

At 11.35 two separate groups of police officers entered the building from different directions. Three officers from one group rushed to the door that Ramos had used to enter, but which was now locked. The police were well armed; the officers all had pistols, and two had rifles. Three officers also wore some sort of protective armour.

Pete Arredondo, the chief of the school district's police department, another school district officer and two Uvalde police officers also got into the building.

Meanwhile, the first group of law enforcement officers approached classrooms 111 and 112. They said that they heard gunfire inside the building and saw a cloud of debris and bullet holes in the walls. Despite this the Texas House Committee said that none of the officers recalled hearing screams or realising children had been shot.

At 11.37 one of the officers, Javier Martinez, peered into the vestibule for rooms 111 and 112. He and another officer faced gunfire and immediately retreated without actually firing a shot.

After retreating, Uvalde Police Lieutenant Javier Martinez moved again toward the hallway, but none of the other officers followed him. According to the *Texas House Committee Report*, several law enforcement officers said that Martinez might have made it to the classroom and engaged with the shooter if others had followed him.

Pete Arredondo called the landline of the Uvalde Police Department to describe the situation. He asked for a SWAT team and a radio. However, unbeknown to him the commander of the Uvalde SWAT team was actually among the first officers to get into the school from the north side of the building.

Sargeant Coronado then asked for shields and flashbangs from the Police Department and helicopter support and ballistic shields from the Texas Department of Public Safety. One of the local officers asked if the door to the classroom was locked. Coronado replied that he did not know, but that the group had a Halligan, an ax-like firefighting tool used to breach doors. The *Texas House Committee Report* said that no officers tested whether the classroom door was locked. Control also asked if there were students inside Room 112 where radio traffic indicated the shooter was, and Coronado responded by requesting a mirror to look around corners. A voice on the radio replied, "class should be in session."

At 11.42 Johnny Field, a Uvalde County constable, arrived and discussed the need to evacuate children. Several officers started breaking classroom windows to evacuate students.

Twenty-one minutes after Ramos entered the school, an onlooker, Angel Ledezma, streamed a live video showing parents begging police to let them enter the school. They were prevented from doing so.

Shootings provoke confusion but the police response can only be described as cowardly. Officers hesitated to go in and confront the killer.

At 11.56 a police officer called Williams said, "There's still kids over here. So, I'm getting the kids out," according to body-camera footage. He later left to continue clearing other classrooms after another officer pointed out to him that his position would create a "crossfire situation."

At 12.03 a student called 911 from Room 112 for 1 minute and 23 seconds and identified herself in a whisper. The *Texas House Committee Report* said it "received no evidence that any officer who did learn about phone calls coming from inside Rooms 111 and 112 acted on it to advocate shifting to an active shooter-style response or otherwise acting more urgently to breach the classrooms."

Meanwhile, at least 19 officers stood in a school hallway. And did nothing.

The student called 911 again at 12.16 saying eight or nine students were alive. Parents tried to break windows but again the police stopped them trying to get in to be reunited with their children.

Fifteen minutes later officers moved closer to Rooms 111 and 112, in preparation for breaking into the classrooms, however, this did not happen at that time.

The student inside the classroom who called 911 begged "Please send the police now."

Finally, officers forced their way in to 112 and killed Ramos, who was hiding in a closet.

The *Texas House Committee Report* criticised officers for taking so long to enter the classroom, saying "there was an unacceptably long period of time before officers breached the classroom, neutralised the attacker, and began rescue efforts."

It went on to say:

> Given the information known about victims who survived through the time of the breach and who later died on the way to the hospital, it is plausible that some victims could have survived if they had not had to wait 73 additional minutes for rescue.

Governor Abbott of Texas called this horror, "incomprehensible"; yet, this attack is both comprehensible and expected in our country because leaders like Governor Abbott have not only refused to take action but actively undermined common-sense laws and solutions that stop these kinds of tragedies.

President Biden was right to ask "when in God's name are we going to stand up to the gun lobby?" as a nation. We have been demanding elected officials to act. We have told lawmakers that preventing gun violence is an "election issue" because it is a life-or-death issue for every American community. "Thoughts and prayers, words and platitudes, are not enough. We need action now."

Therapeutic interventions

Psychologists tried to help. A team from the University of Texas at Austin came on-site to help. The team worked at a walk-in clinic.

Children were disoriented, confused, frantic and panicky, while others seemed emotionally shut down – not surprising, since sometimes trauma symptoms don't really hit until 3–6 months later.

The main approach the team used was psychological first aid, an intervention developed by the National Child Traumatic Stress Network.

"We're trying to do a whole-person assessment – to determine risk factors for each individual child," one of the therapists Shail Jani said. A whole-person assessment includes factors related to the trauma itself – whether the child was actually on-site or heard about the incident second-hand, for example – and other factors like family environment and previous levels of trauma.

In the last 20 years studies of trauma have looked at what makes for resilience. Being part of a faith group was shown to help as did spending time with friends or engaging in other pleasurable activities.

A series of photographs in the *New Yorker* show sad children waiting at a bus stop to go to the school. The trauma seems very much with them.

It is not as if law enforcement has made no attempt to understand. The United States Secret Service National Threat Assessment Center's "Protecting America's Schools/Analysis of Targeted School Violence/2019" studied

41 incidents of school violence between 2008 and 2017. The analysis suggested that many of these tragedies could have been prevented, and recommended the threshold for intervention should be low, so that schools can identify students in distress before they became dangerous. The report pointed to many other problems. It argued:

- There is no profile of a student attacker, nor is there a profile for the type of school that has been targeted: Attackers varied in age, gender, race, grade level, academic performance, and social characteristics. Attackers usually had multiple motives, the most common involving a grievance with classmates: In addition to grievances with classmates, attackers were also motivated by grievances involving school staff, romantic relationships, or other personal issues. Other motives included a desire to kill, suicide, and seeking fame or notoriety. Discovering a student's motive for engaging in concerning behaviour is critical to assessing the student's risk of engaging in violence and identifying appropriate interventions to change behaviour and manage risk.
- Most attackers had experienced psychological, behavioural, or developmental symptoms: Their mental health symptoms were divided into three main categories: psychological (e.g., depressive symptoms or suicidal ideation), behavioural (e.g., defiance/misconduct or symptoms of ADHD), and neurological/developmental (e.g., developmental delays or cognitive deficits).

  Half of the attackers had interests in violent topics. The reports said such interests are worrying and schools should not hesitate to initiate further information-gathering, assessment and management of the student's behaviour. Schools should take note of any student who is preoccupied with Hitler or the Columbine shooting.

  In the six months before they killed, and often in the 48 hours before the killing, all attackers experienced social stressors involving their relationships with peers and/or romantic partners and academic issues. All school personnel should be trained to recognise signs of a student in crisis.
- Nearly every attacker experienced problems at home including parental separation or divorce, drug use or criminal charges among family members, and domestic abuse. Most attackers were victims of bullying, which was often observed by others: It is critical that schools implement comprehensive programs designed to promote safe and positive school climates, where students feel empowered to report bullying when they witness it or are victims of it, and where school officials and other authorities act to intervene.
- Most attackers had been in trouble at school and with the police. The attacker was suspended, expelled, cautioned or arrested because of their behaviour at school. An important point for school staff to consider is that punitive measures are not preventative. If a student elicits concern or poses a risk of harm to self or others, removing the student from the school may not always be the safest option.

Most of the attackers communicated a prior threat to their target or communicated their intentions to carry out an attack. In many cases, someone observed a threatening communication or behaviour but did not act, either out of fear, not believing the attacker, misjudging the immediacy or location, or believing they had dissuaded the attacker.

A thorough review of the findings contained in this report should make clear that we know much about the shooters but still do not know how to stop them.

The US seems to have exported the problem. In Thailand a former police officer, 34-year-old Panya Kamrap, who had been sacked for drug use, killed at least 37 people in a shooting and stabbing rampage that started at a childcare centre in north-east Thailand in October 2022.

Police Major General Paisal Luesomboon said that after he fled, the gunman continued to shoot from his car, hitting several people.

After the attack Kamrap killed his wife and child at home. And then shot himself. His case has some similarities to domestic cases.

There is a clear motive in domestic cases – nearly always jealousy or fear of loss. School killings have no such obvious cause. These tragedies make us feel powerless – powerless to stop such events and powerless to understand why some people want to die enough to kill? The other question is why are we unable to pin down why agencies so often fail to act when there have been many warning signs? There seems to be no end to school killings. Children in Serbia have been victims in May 2023. Mercy and reason lose out again and again.

9 Poverty, class and social work

Just as the police often fail in their duties in mass shootings, agencies have a dismal record of failing children, especially poor children in working-class families. Many reports highlight a lack of professional curiosity as parents fob off authorities (who should be on guard against this) and children suffer. Poor children are at greater risk of death from all kinds of causes. In 2020–21, 3.9 million children lived in poverty in the UK, a dismaying 27 per cent of children. So, their already vulnerable parents may often face another trauma.

The history of the Battered Baby Syndrome is telling. In Victorian London babies were often killed, but psychologists ignored the issue. Then in the 1940s and 50s radiologists in Britain and America, used x-ray technology to "make visible" children's injuries. In England, the National Society for the prevention of Cruelty to Children (NSPCC) drew on this work to conduct early studies about the Battered Child Syndrome.

John Caffey (1965), Frederic Silverman (1953) and Paul Woolley and William Evans's (1955) research (https://www.ncbi.nlm.nih.gov/books/NBK535578) highlighted the tragedy that parents can have deliberately injured children and were some of the first to discuss parental violence in the medical press. Caffey wrote that the fractures he observed "appear to be of traumatic origin." Silverman argued that parents may "permit trauma and be unaware of it, may recognize trauma but forget or be reluctant to admit it, or may deliberately injure the child and deny it." Woolley and Evans also diagnosed the "aggressive, immature or emotionally ill" characters of certain parents. These assertions were relatively tentative but nevertheless they urged doctors to look for signs and explanations for what had happened, especially fractures, soft tissue swellings and skin bruising.

In 1984, Kempe published "The Battered Child Syndrome," in the *Journal of the American Medical Association* choosing the dramatic term "battered child," he later commented, as a "jazzy title, designed to get physicians' attention."

Kempe described the "Battered Child Syndrome" as a "clinical condition in young children," usually under the age of three though possibly of "any age," who had been subject to serious physical violence. The NSPCC established a new unit to research battered children, which also focused on the psychological characteristics of violent parents.

DOI: 10.4324/9781003272670-9

Britain saw the first of many highly publicised cases of battered children in 1974 with the death of Maria Colwell. In the next 30 years there were many more deaths, many more reports but not much action. I interviewed Brian Ryaged, the director of social services in Newcastle, who was unhappy at the fact that his profession had often missed instances of child cruelty.

Then in August 2007, 17-month-old Peter Connelly was found dead in his cot after he had been beaten and had cigarettes stubbed out on his body. His mother, Tracey, her boyfriend, Steven Barker, and his brother, Jason Owen, were convicted of "causing or allowing" Peter's death.

Baby P had suffered more than 50 injuries. Over eight months he had been seen 60 times by social workers from Haringey Council, doctors and police. His death took place only a few years after that of Victoria Climbié, aged eight, which had also involved Haringey Council.

A serious case review published in 2010 found every agency involved in the care of Baby P – GPs, hospitals, the police and social services – had been "well motivated" and wanted to protect him. But they were collectively and individually "completely inadequate." They had often failed to challenge the mother's explanations for her son's injuries.

The Sun newspaper decided to launch a "Baby P" campaign, labelling it a "fight for justice" and called for the sacking of all those involved at Haringey. Ed Balls, then education secretary, ordered the removal of Haringey's director of social services live on TV. A climate of fear gripped social workers as a "Baby P effect" triggered a surge in child protection referrals and children being taken into care.

Gillie Christou, a team manager in the Haringey child protection service responsible for Baby P's case, was at the centre of the storm.

She said,

> hearing that a child you've been working with has died is among the worst news any social worker can get. . . .
>
> I still remember the shock I felt. How had this happened? Why this child of all the others I had responsibility for? It was unexpected. Initially there was confusion about how Peter had died. It may be hard to believe, but at that time there was no talk of serious injury and the question of 'how' still needed to be answered. I had no idea how to react.

That was a difficult but honest admission.

In August 2009, Haringey told Christou she would be sacked along with the other social care staff involved in the case. Nine months later she was told that the then social work regulator, the General Social Care Council, would report its findings of a long investigation into the fitness to practise of Christou and Maria Ward, who had been Peter's allocated social worker. The investigation found both social workers had made mistakes which amounted to misconduct. They failed to keep adequate records. Ward had not visited Peter often enough. Christou had failed to provide enough supervision. However, Christou and

Ward were both just suspended from practising. Their errors were not serious enough for them to be struck off.

In 2009, the then Labour government published the findings of the Social Work Taskforce, which led to the creation of the Social Work Reform Board and the College of Social Work in a bid to boost the profession's status. By this time the media were focusing attention on high caseloads, inadequate IT systems and problems with the recruitment and retention of social workers.

When the Conservative and Liberal Democrat coalition came to power in 2010, it commissioned Professor Eileen Munro, a former social worker and academic at the London School of Economics, to carry out a thorough review of child protection. She found social services had become too obsessed with complying with procedures and regulations – the Ticking Boxes Syndrome. Munro said:

> The broader public sector was gripped by new public management at the time and the idea that top down control was the way to do it. It was called the 'targets and terror' approach. When you apply that to the child protection field, which has enough terror anyway because of the horror of a child dying, then it really was quite damaging. . . .
>
> I was really quite disturbed by how many social workers talked about families they were working with in a very bureaucratic, rather than a human way. Somebody was a 'section 47' rather than a woman who is living with four children in an appalling house who is trying her hardest but making a bit of a mess of it.
>
> If you don't make that human contact with a person then you can't help solve their problems. At least, to me, that's what social work is about. But social work had become about processing and referring-on, not helping.
>
> (Munro, 2011)

Munro set out a blueprint for a "child-centred" system which would help create the conditions to help professionals make the best judgements they could to protect a child.

Despite the furore about Baby P the system still sees children suffer.

The tragedies behind the figures can be found in the *NSPCC Digest* (2022). What follows is a summary of some of the cases in which children died. I must add that on the several occasions that I rang the NSPCC they did not reply.

2022 – Anonymous – Charley

The murder of a young child by their mother's partner.

The NSPCC judged the case showed the need to improve work with fathers and blamed a decision to cease multi-agency planning without considering the risks of children being exposed to escalating harm without adequate review mechanisms. No assessment that considers risk of domestic abuse should be accepted as complete without exhausting all options and that had to include the alleged perpetrator of the abuse.

2022 – Anonymous – Child G

Attempted suicide by a 7-year-old child at the family home. Sixteen months earlier Child G had disclosed that they had been sexually abused on two occasions by their stepfather.

The NSPCC judged it was important to continue to communicate with children about their world; professionals needed to think about what might be a change in the child's priorities rather than adhere exclusively to an adult assumption of what the child requires; they should consider a more judicious use of care planning forums when there was lack of clarity about what the options are in reducing risk within families; there should be more effective planning, assessment and recording at all stages of a case.

2018 – Anonymous – Pippa

Death of a 15-year-old girl in September 2018 by suicide. Pippa was subject to a care order and lived in a care home at the time of her death.

The NSPCC decided the case showed the importance of considering how childhood experiences can impact the behaviour and vulnerabilities of troubled adolescents. Practitioners needed to assess and engage with all significant men in a child's life; where child sexual exploitation was suspected, risk assessments needed to consider any possibilities which emerge of past abuse, loss and trauma; professionals needed to maintain a questioning and curious response to what they were told or saw; a lack of knowledge among professionals about the evidence base related to risk indicators for adolescent suicide could leave them ill-equipped to discuss or recognise signs and respond accordingly.

2022 – Hampshire – Child P

Death of a 5-week-old infant in 2019 due to severe, widespread and irreversible brain injury. Both parents were arrested and subject to criminal investigations. Mother was subsequently convicted of manslaughter.

Yet again the NSPCC noted agencies needed to share information and assessment of risk; professionals needed to guard against over optimism and maintain professional curiosity especially if drugs were involved.

2022 – Gloucester – Ella and Laura

Joint domestic homicide review and serious case review. Murder of an 11-year-old girl, Ella, by her stepfather in May 2018. Ella's mother, Laura, was also murdered.

The NSPCC concluded it was important to keep in mind the role of family and friends as a source of support; the need to consider the voice of the child; the impact of a new step-parent and his or her background on a child's life. Professionals needed to know and document who has parental responsibility for a child as well as the other adults in a child's life. Services should ensure they had proper policy, training and record-keeping procedures to adequately address domestic abuse, and compare themselves against best practice or national guidance; all frontline professionals need to speak confidentially to survivors of domestic abuse about their situation despite any denial or minimisation, to understand where barriers come from and to address domestic abuse beyond basic inquiry.

2022 – Hampshire – Emma

Death of a 16-year-old girl, Emma who was staying with a relative at the time of her death. The relative's partner was convicted of Emma's murder and sentenced to life imprisonment.

Emma's positive presentation may have resulted in professional over-optimism and disguised her ongoing vulnerability, the NSPCC concluded. The supporting professional network needed to consider the parent's ability to support the child; when children are linked to exploitation it should be established if the parent is able to understand the risk posed by contextual safeguarding issues.

Recommendations included encouraging practitioners to operate a reflective mind-set with their case work, being aware of over-optimism and ensuring continuing practice of professional curiosity.

2019 – Darwen, Lancashire – Millie

Suicide of an 11-year-old-girl, Millie, in March 2019. The NSPCC advocated being less risk adverse and more risk sensible about working together; demonstrating professional curiosity about the effect an absent parent or role model may have on the well-being of a child; thinking about the bigger picture and adopting a single, whole-system approach to the needs and risk of a child; being alert to the impact that an increase in the number of underlying risk indicators can have on a child and being able to spot them, and then responding to them collectively, as early as possible, even in the absence of any obvious high risk factors.

Mariano, Chan and Myers (2014) found that about 15 per cent of homicide arrests over a 32-year period were of a filicidal nature.

Research studies have identified five possible motives adults who murder children might have. The *Altruistic group* includes parents who believe they killed their child to put an end to real or imagined suffering. The *Acutely Psychotic group* includes those who killed for some irrational motive. The *Unwanted*

Child group view their child as a hindrance. The *Fatal Maltreatment group* encompasses parents whose children died as an unintended consequence of neglect or abuse. Finally, the fifth category, the *Spousal Revenge group* is reserved for those parents who kill a child in order to get back at a spouse or partner.

The question that needs to be asked is, "How do parents get to a point where they inflict such cruelty on their own flesh and blood?"

10 The physical consequences of bereavement

Definitions affect cash flow. Grief is neither a disease nor is it classified as a mental disorder, and the main US funding agency, the National Institutes of Health, has no single established channel for funding research into grief. The reason that scientists do not know more about the biology of grief is because few researchers get the backing to study it, and they are usually psychologists with biological interests.

In a study of the long-term impact of bereavement upon spouse health Jones, Bartrop, Forcier and Penny (2010) found that bereaved spouses were more likely to die prematurely than individuals with mental health or circulation problems.

Why this happens is less clear, possibly because of the difficulties in conducting research at a time of great distress. Proposed explanations for the increased risk in bereaved individuals include the tendency of unfit people to marry similarly unfit spouses, and the possibility that the spouses may share with the bereaved the same poor environment and dietary and social factors. Various studies have adjusted for bias from socio-economic, environmental and common lifestyles, accidents shared with spouses, age, ethnicity and education. It is therefore plausible that much of the increased health risk stems from the impact of psychological grief reactions on, and with, physiological responses, which make the early phases of bereavement so harrowing and tough.

Surprisingly little is known about the effect of parental bereavement on something as basic as physical health. One exception is a Danish study by Murphy, Johnson, Wu, Fan and Lohan (2003) who investigated whether the death of a child increased mortality in parents. They studied 21,062 parents in Denmark who lost a child and 293,745 controls – i.e., parents whose children were alive.

Mothers died from unnatural causes throughout follow-up, with the highest rate recorded during the first three years of bereavement. Bereaved fathers had only an early excess mortality from unnatural causes.

Murphy et al. (2003) observed 173 parents 4, 12, 24 and 60 months after the death of their child by accident, suicide or homicide. They examined the

DOI: 10.4324/9781003272670-10

influence of three types of violent death of a child and the time since death on mental distress, PTSD, acceptance of the child's death and marital satisfaction. Nearly 70 per cent of the parents reported that it took between three and four years to put their children's death into perspective and continue with their own lives; however, the cause of the child's death did not significantly influence how long it took parents to recover. The trauma of losing a child can trigger physical symptoms, including stomach pains, muscle cramps, headaches and even Irritable Bowel Syndrome. A handful of studies have found more tenuous links between what the researchers call "unresolved" grief and immune disorders, cancer and long-term genetic changes at the cellular level.

Krisch (2019) noted that 84 per cent of mothers reported low or moderate physical well-being (far higher than the 45 per cent of fathers who reported this). Mothers were also significantly more likely to be on medication or have taken sick leave while fathers were more likely to report sleep problems and nightmares. One reason could be that mothers still spend more time with their children during the day, on average, while fathers tend to spend more time working. It is possible that men feel the loss most acutely in the evenings, when work is finished, their minds are clear and there is no child to play with.

In 2017, Frank Infurna and Suniya Luthar studied 461 parents who had lost children over 13 years. They reported, "We did see some decline, followed by a general bounce-back, or recovery, over time." Infurna and Luthar found little decline in the ability to complete various everyday tasks – "we didn't see much change in this." However when bereaved parents were asked to report on their well-being, on whether they felt they got sick often or whether they expected their health to improve or decline they were more pessimistic.

Inevitably there is a medical term which is not jargon laden, the Broken Heart Syndrome; it has many of the symptoms of a textbook heart attack. They include crushing chest pain, and it is not just the heart that is affected. A new study recently found potential mechanisms that may contribute to Broken Heart Syndrome; it was led by investigators at Massachusetts General Hospital (MGH). A heart–brain connection likely plays a major role.

The team analyzed brain imaging scans from 104 patients (41 who subsequently developed the condition and 63 who did not) to determine whether increased stress-associated metabolic activity in the brain leads to an elevated risk of developing heart problems. "Areas of the brain that have higher metabolic activity tend to be in greater use. Hence, higher activity in the stress-associated centers of the brain suggests that the individual has a more active response to stress," according to Ahmed Tawakol, director of Nuclear Cardiology and co-director of the Cardiovascular Imaging Research Center at MGH.

The imaging tests, which were being conducted in patients for other medical reasons, revealed that heightened activity in the brain's amygdala predicted the development of subsequent broken heart symptoms, as well as the timing of the syndrome. Individuals who had the highest amygdalar activity developed the condition within a year after imaging, while those with intermediate values developed it several years later. Tawakol says:

We show that TTS or Takotsubo cardiomyopathy (as is the technical term), happens not only because one encounters a rare, dreadfully disturbing event—such as the death of a spouse or child, as the classical examples have it. Rather, individuals with high stress-related brain activity appear to be primed to develop the condition—and can develop the syndrome upon exposure to more common stressors, even a routine colonoscopy or a bone fracture says Tawakol.

He hopes that interventions that lower stress-related brain activity will make it more difficult to develop TTS. "Studies should test whether such approaches to decrease stress-associated brain activity decrease the chance that TTS will recur among patients with prior episodes of TTS," he says. He also underscores the need for more studies into the impact of stress reduction – or drug interventions targeting stress-related brain activity – on heart health.

Chris Fagundes, a psychologist at Rice University, Texas, and his team have found links between grief, depression and changes to the immune and cardiovascular systems (Fagundes, 2020). In 2019, he and his team assessed 99 bereaved people about three months after the deaths of their spouses, and then took blood samples. Those who experienced higher levels of grief and depression also had higher levels of the immune system's markers for inflammation.

"Chronic inflammation can be dangerous," Dr Fagundes said. "It can contribute to cardiovascular disease, Type 2 diabetes, some cancers." In an earlier study, published in 2018, Fagundes and his colleagues found that bereaved spouses who had higher levels of markers for inflammation also had what experts refer to as lower heart rate variability. The physiology is well understood.

The autonomic nervous system (ANS) controls heart rate. The ANS, which is divided into two components, the sympathetic and the parasympathetic nervous system, regulates heart rate, blood pressure, digestion and breathing. These two components are referred to as the fight-or-flight system and the relaxation response.

The hypothalamus, a small region above the brain stem, constantly processes information and transmits signals to the rest of the body through the ANS. The signals can either relax or stimulate different functions in the body, including the heart rate which can go into overdrive under stress.

Although the ANS influences the rate at which your heart beats, the heart beats on its rhythm because of the sinoatrial node (SA node), a natural pacemaker that keeps it beating at around 100 beats per minute. Under stress the heart beats faster.

Hopf et al. (2020), found that people who scored higher on psychological measures of grief also had higher levels of certain stress hormones like cortisol and epinephrine. Over time, chronic stress can increase the risk of cardiovascular conditions as well as diabetes, cancer, autoimmune conditions and depression and anxiety.

Research suggests the brain is key. It responds to the death (and to intense stress in general), by releasing certain hormones that fan out into the body, affecting the cardiovascular system and the cells of the immune system. This is a rather general statement but the biology of grief has no clear chain of cause-and-effect in the way that the biology of, say, diabetes, does.

Some of the most thorough research is Scandinavian. A study led by Dr Krisztina László at the Karolinska Institute, Stockholm, found an association between the loss of a close family member and an increased risk of mortality from heart failure occurring after the death of a child, partner, grandchild or sibling but not the death of a parent. The mortality risk after any loss was greatest in the first week after bereavement.

Laszlo's work reported in *Medical News Today* (July 22, 2022) and that of Chen and others (Chen et al., 2022) is based on patient records between 2000 and 2018 from the Swedish Heart Failure Registry and data from between 1987 and 2018 from the Swedish Patient Register. The total sample was very large, almost 500,000 individuals.

One of the findings is very surprising. The greatest risk of mortality was observed after the loss of a partner (20 per cent) or a sibling (13 per cent). Researchers only observed a 10 per cent increased mortality risk after the death of a child and a 5 per cent increased risk after the loss of a grandchild.

Dr László said, "The findings of the study may call for increased attention from family members, friends, and involved professionals for bereaved heart failure patients, particularly in the period shortly after the loss."

László explained it was important to understand the underlying causes of the increased risk and "whether less severe sources of stress may also contribute to poor prognosis in heart failure."

Dr Suzanne Steinbaum (2016), cardiologist and American Heart Association Trusted Source volunteer, explained:

> People with heart failure need to be aware of their own increased risk of mortality after losing a family member. Being empowered with this knowledge can help provide a strategy to protect themselves and their hearts by scheduling visits to their healthcare providers, finding social support during this difficult time, and ensuring that they continue to monitor and care for themselves, especially during the grieving process.

She added that people tend to focus on their grief, more than on their own well-being. After losing a loved one, "it is critically important to reach out to your healthcare provider to ensure that one's own survival is not put in jeopardy during the grieving process."

However, it is not only the heart that is stricken.

The gut

In the nine years since Reuben died I have lost 9 kilos, mainly because about two years ago I stopped stuffing myself with pasta. Food offers comfort. One study (Brattico et al., 2011) involved showing sad images and music to people while in a magnetic resonance imaging (MRI) scanner. One group had fats injected into their stomachs, while the other group had a saline placebo. Because they didn't actually ingest the food, no pleasure or flavour was involved in eating; however, those with the fat injections showed they were 50 per cent less saddened by the images and music.

(Pathways 2023)

You grieve and think I've just lost my loved one . . . why should I care any more? Why *not* eat that box of cookies? And kind friends often bring fruit baskets, cookie bouquets, cakes, pies and casseroles, which all start to pile up.

Heartache can make the belly ache but research examining the connection between bereavement stress and gut health is limited. Van Oudenhove et al. (2011) found an interaction between fatty acid infusion and emotion induction both in mood and hunger. Specifically, the behavioral and neural responses to sad emotion induction were attenuated by fatty acid infusion. Chronic and ongoing stress can disrupt the microbiome.

According to Thalia Hale, as quoted in a *Time Magazine* article in 2022, grief upsets the gastrointestinal tract.

Stress can activate the sympathetic nervous system, more commonly known as the fight-or-flight response. In this state, "heart rate and blood pressure rise, as do levels of the hormone cortisol," Hale says. And when the body is warding off danger, it's not focused on digestion or eating.

Suicide

The literature on suicide in bereaved parents in general is scant.

A recent Danish population study (Li et al., 2003) showed twice as many deaths by suicide in bereaved mothers compared with a matched cohort of mothers who had not lost a child. The data did not, however, link the mother's suicide with her child's cause of death. Generally, being a parent protects against suicide. But the death of a child strongly affected parental suicide, and the impact was greater when adjusted for other risk factors. Death of a young child (1–6 years) was correlated with a greater number of suicides in parents, and the risk was highest the month after the death of the child.

Some parents cannot cope with the death of a child. Davies (2006) reports two cases of suicide.

Case 1

A boy with a congenital rhabdoid tumour of the face received palliative care at home for progressive disease. The tumour grew to involve almost half of his face. He presented with pain seven weeks before his death. Initially the pain was controlled with codeine and simple analgesics, but it gradually intensified. He was then treated with morphine.

Two days before his death, he developed sudden signs of obstruction to his airway. He had been prescribed Lorazepam in anticipation of such an event. This was titrated until it helped. He was sleepy but could be roused, and he no longer seemed anxious, despite visibly laboured breathing.

A paediatric palliative care nurse saw him two hours before he died. Although he still had laboured breathing, he slept peacefully. He died the day before his first birthday. His mother refused to have his body removed from the home the night of his death and declined to have a nurse come to the home to help. The next day, in a lengthy visit, a paediatric home care nurse tried but failed to have the parents release the body to a funeral parlour. They also refused to return the baby's drugs to the pharmacy. The parents repeatedly denied any suicide plans, and said they would return the drugs later.

The oncology and palliative care doctors involved, the managers of the home care nursing, the crisis unit and the coroner were contacted. A decision was made not to intervene again until the next day. A particular decision was made not to admit the mother to hospital against her wishes, given her denial of suicidal intent, and not to force removal of her son's body from the home. It seemed to be important to the mother that her baby's body was there on his birthday.

The mother was found unconscious the next morning by her partner and was pronounced dead upon arrival at hospital.

Case 2

An 8-year-old girl received palliative care services at home for advanced metastatic Wilms's disease.

Days after her death, her mother was found unconscious at home. She had taken the child's enteral methadone. The family had been advised to return all drugs to the pharmacy on the day that their child died by the home care nurse who visited them. The parents had stopped answering telephone calls from the palliative care nurse and home care nurses after the child's death. The mother was admitted to a hospital's intensive care unit, and she survived.

Our brain controls us, defines us even.

The brain

Chronic stress can affect how the brain functions, as long-term exposure to the stress hormone cortisol has been linked to the death of brain cells. In a cruel twist of neurobiology, the key regions for grief, such as the posterior cingulate cortex, frontal cortex and cerebellum, are also involved in regulating appetite and sleep.

"There are many, many studies that have looked at the ongoing health effects of high levels of chronic stress," Gail Saltz, a psychiatrist at the New York Presbyterian Hospital Weill-Cornell School of Medicine, told me in an interview. "And when you look at lists of stressful life events, this is at the top."

Mary-Frances O'Connor, a psychologist at the University of Arizona, studies both the psychology of grief and its biological changes in the laboratory and is one of the few researchers who straddle both fields. Hybrid science is seldom well funded. She has been influenced by the work of George Bonanno who coined the term *the new science of bereavement*. O'Connor also examines the loss of a job, a pet and even the pain we feel when a celebrity whom we admire but have never met dies.

In 2001, O'Connor began imaging the grieving brain, and a handful of similar studies have been done since. In these studies, a person lies still in an MRI scanner. I know from irritating personal experience that this is not so easy. When I was put in one my left leg kept wobbling. The operator became impatient and after 15 minutes of me trying to control my leg he gave up. The papers I have read do not mention such hiccups, if a leg can have hiccups.

O'Connor's work asked the still-as-a-log patient to look at certain pictures and listen to certain words while the MRI mapped the blood flow to parts of the brain. Three areas of the brain were triggered by words related to grief (like "funeral" or "loss") and a fourth triggered by pictures of the person who died. Some of the brain areas were usually involved in the experience of pain, others in having autobiographical memories.

The responses recorded in another area, called the *nucleus accumbens*, were more surprising. This region is part of the brain's network for reward, the part that responds to, say, chocolate. What was remarkable was that it was active only in people with complicated grief. Dr O'Connor suggested that being reminded of a loved one with pictures and words might offer the same reward as seeing a living loved one. In uncomplicated grieving, the reminder is no longer connected "to a living reward but is understood as a memory of someone no longer here."

In *The Grieving Brain* (2022) O'Connor has summed up years of research.

The brain is, among many other things, an organ that solves puzzles. O'Connor eventually realised the brain has to solve a problem when a loved one dies. Losing someone we need and love is in some ways like being deprived of food and water.

The brain often prefers habits and predictions over new information. But it struggles to learn new information even if that information cannot be ignored, like the absence of our loved one. O'Connor compares this to a kind of learning, as we have to discard the map we have used to navigate our lives together with the loved one. Grieving, or learning to live a meaningful life without our loved one, is ultimately a type of learning. She argues that as we learn all our lives, seeing grieving as a type of learning may make it feel more familiar and understandable, and give us the patience to allow it to unfold.

O'Connor wrote,

When I talk to students or clinicians or even people sitting next to me on a plane, I find they have burning questions about grief. They ask: Is grief the same as depression? When people do not show their grief, is it because they are in denial? Is losing a child worse than losing a spouse? Then, very often, they ask me this type of question: I know someone whose mom/

brother/best friend/husband died, and after six weeks/four months/eighteen months/ten years, they still feel grief. Is this normal?

She argues that grief researchers have not been very successful at broadcasting what they have learned and how new methods allow us to look inside the brain, which tantalises us with possible answers to ancient questions. She is careful not to overclaim.

> I do not believe that a neuroscientific perspective on grief is any better than a sociological, a religious, or an anthropological one. I say that genuinely, despite devoting an entire career to the neurobiological lens. I believe our understanding of grief through a neurobiological lens can enhance our understanding, create a more holistic view of grief, and help us engage in new ways with the anguish and terror of what grief is like.

She distinguishes between grief and *grieving*. Grief is the intense emotion that crashes over you like a wave. You cannot ignore it. Grief is a moment that recurs over and over. Grief never ends, and it is a natural response to loss. You will experience pangs of grief over a specific person forever. You will have moments that overwhelm you, even years after the death when you have restored your life to a meaningful, fulfilling experience. But whereas you will feel the universally human emotion of grief forever, your grieving – which includes how you adapt to the way you do it – changes over time. The first one hundred times you have a wave of grief, you may think, I will never get through this, I cannot bear this. The one hundred and first time, you may think, I hate this, I don't want this – but it is familiar, and I know I will get through this moment. Even if the feeling of grief is the same, your relationship to the feeling changes. Feeling grief years after your loss may make you doubt whether you have really adapted. If you think of the emotion and the process of adaptation as two different things, however, then it isn't a problem that you experience *grief* even when you have been *grieving* for a long time.

You can think about our journey together through this book as a series of mysteries. O'Connor's book, *The Grieving Brain*, raises obvious questions.

Why do we ruminate so much after we lose a loved one? Changing what we spend our time thinking about can change our neural connections and increase our chances of learning to live a meaningful life. Why would we engage in our life in the present moment, if it is full of grief? The answer for her is clear as it is only in the present moment that we can also experience joy and common humanity, and express love to our living loved ones.

Finally, O'Connor asks, "How can our grief ever change, if the person will never return?" Our brain is remarkable, it enables us to imagine an infinite number of future possibilities. She considers what cognitive psychology can contribute to our understanding of grieving and what may make the winding path of grieving more familiar and hopeful.

She identifies three factors involved in grieving. First the brain is central, built from centuries of evolution and hundreds of thousands of hours "of your own personal experience with love and loss." The second character is bereavement science, a young field full of charismatic scientists and clinicians, as well as the false starts and exciting discoveries of any scientific endeavour. Finally, she hopes "you may see through a new lens how your brain enables you to carry your loved one with you through the rest of your life."

All of the studies mentioned have limitations. Many of them use small samples and have not been replicated. Many are also a snapshot of one point in time and will miss the changes that occur in most people over months and years. Studies using MRI scans have limits all of their own, too: "A lot of things could make the same areas light up," Dr O'Connor writes, "and the same thing might not make the same areas light up in everyone or in one person over time."

Grief, both biological and psychological, is of course the result of another hard-to-study state, human attachment or love. "Humans are predisposed to form loving bonds," Dr O'Connor writes, "and as soon as you do, your body is loaded and cocked for what happens when that person is gone. So, all systems that functioned well now must accommodate the person's absence." For most people, the systems adjust: "Our bodies are amazingly resilient."

Psychology prides itself on making advances and researchers have now discovered, or perhaps devised, a new category of grief which is even more traumatic.

Complicated grief

There are many tests of grief and sometimes one is astonished by the persistence of testers. Some of the instruments, as testers often refer to their tests, include the 30-item ICG-R Test (Prigerson and Jacobs, 2001a), the Dutch version of the *Inventory of Traumatic Grief* (Boelen et al., 2003), the *Traumatic Grief Evaluation of Response to Loss* (Prigerson and Jacobs, 2001b) as well as structured interviews which explore individual responses.

Symptoms of avoidance, hyper-arousal and intrusion can be scored using the 22-item Impact of Event Scale – Revised (IES-R) (1997).

Other signs and symptoms of complicated grief may include:

- Intense sorrow, pain and rumination over the loss of your loved one
- Focus on little else but your loved one's death
- Extreme focus on reminders of the loved one or excessive avoidance of reminders
- Intense and persistent longing or pining for the deceased
- Problems accepting the death
- Numbness or detachment
- Bitterness about your loss
- Feeling that life holds no meaning or purpose
- Lack of trust in others
- Inability to enjoy life or think back on positive experiences with your loved one.

Other signs of complicated grief are continuing to:

- Have trouble carrying out normal routines
- Isolate from others and withdraw from social activities
- Experience depression, deep sadness, guilt or self-blame
- Believe that you did something wrong or could have prevented the death
- Feel life isn't worth living without your loved one
- Wish you had died along with your loved one.

No one knows yet what causes complicated grief, but likely causes are:

- Death of a child
- Close or dependent relationship on the deceased person
- Social isolation or loss of a support system or friendships
- Past history of depression, separation anxiety or PTSD
- Traumatic childhood experiences, such as abuse or neglect
- Other major life stressors, such as major financial hardships.

Without appropriate treatment, complications may include:

- Depression
- Suicidal thoughts or behaviours
- Anxiety, including PTSD
- Significant sleep disturbances
- Increased risk of physical illness, such as heart disease, cancer or high blood pressure
- Long-term difficulty with daily living, relationships or work activities
- Alcohol, nicotine use or substance misuse.

Breathing is an area less studied though it is vital.

> Different emotions change our breathing patterns and since grief triggers a range of emotions, our breathing pattern can get stuck and become inconsistent impacting on our health long term. When we are stressed, our breathing rate increases and the rhythm and the muscles we use to breathe also change. Long term, these changes together with our posture and activation of our flight, fright and freeze muscles keep us lodged in these patterns and unable to move through the stages of grief.
>
> Learning how to change your posture, release stress muscles and change the way you breathe can all help unravel the impacts grief has on your mind and nervous system. For those wanting a simple tool to help release tense muscles changing your posture, not getting slumped, does unwind those overactive stress muscles, making it easier to breathe in a calm state.
>
> (Lettieri, 2021)

What may help is not surprising and some suggestions for dealing with it are not surprising either.

The given view is that talking about your grief and allowing yourself to cry also can help prevent you from getting stuck in your sadness. There is as we shall see some evidence for this but talking is not healing.

The psychiatrist Richard Lettieri (2021) described an American case.

> Janice intentionally killed her 11-month-old daughter Kimberly. A 911 dispatcher took a call from a desperate woman. "I just stabbed my daughter."
>
> The incredulous dispatcher, asked, "You did what?"
>
> "Please," Janice squealed. "Help!"
>
> At her trial the jury decided that Janice was sane at the time of the stabbing, even after two experts, Letterl and the prosecution's own expert, argued that she was insane. Two prison psychiatrists also testified that she was psychotic at that time.
>
> Kimberly was dead before she arrived at the hospital. Janice had many self-inflicted stab wounds, including deep slashes to her chest.
>
> It was a week after the infanticide before she was stable enough to be fully interviewed by the police at the hospital. During one interview, a detective asked Janice a series of questions. "You stabbed her, right?" A moment later, "You knew it was wrong, right?"
>
> She was either unresponsive or off-topic, mumbling something about her husband Richard. "I begged him," she said.
>
> "What about the knife?" the detective asked.
>
> Janice replied, "I didn't want to hurt my baby. I wanted to save my family . . . he was torturing us."
>
> When asked if she stabbed Kimberly to get even with Richard, Janice reacted, "God no. He wanted it this way. I begged him."
>
> The detective persisted. "So, you were mad at him?"
>
> Janice blurted out, "Are you listening. No!"
>
> During a later interview, she was more articulate and revealed her paranoia. Referring to her husband, she said "I had scary thoughts . . . Richard was taking my daughter away . . . I heard him threaten to put me six feet under . . . he was gonna hurt me and my baby . . ."

Lettieri diagnosed Janice with major depression and psychosis.

> I also noted that there was no evidence of her faking or exaggerating her symptoms. It was also clear from interviews with Janice and family members, and the results of psychological testing, that Janice and Richard's marriage had been sound for years and that, as she descended into psychosis, he was concerned, supportive and reached out to the family for help.

The suffering is not just physical.

11 Psychological research

In complicated families there is so much to do after a death. I told Julia about Reuben's death, who said she would light candles for him. I have described the immediate aftermath. It has often been claimed that having to make funeral arrangements helps distracts from the pain. Aileen's sisters, Adele and Amelie, flew over from America. I went to meet them at Manchester Airport. Both loved Reuben. As I waited for them, there was a Hassid standing near me and I told him what had happened. He offered to pray for Reuben. Kindness, but useless kindness.

We took a cab back to New Brighton. Adele and Amelie wanted to know what had happened. Aileen felt her sisters were in another, and very alien world, which was of course true.

We had to arrange the funeral. We knew Reuben would have wanted a Jewish funeral. A rabbi we knew gave us the name of an undertaker who arranged it. We discovered there was a Jewish cemetery in Liverpool. I told Julia about Reuben's death, and she said she would light candles for him. She and Alex did that.

Reuben died at a time when I had money problems. The funeral was going to cost over £4000. I did not have the cash and found myself having to ask friends for short-term help. I was lucky; two of them immediately responded generously.

Having been paid, the undertaker got to work. The mechanics of the body are not something you want to think about. The post-mortem done, Reuben's body was released though we did not see it. Officialdom takes over. The undertakers must have collected it and embalmed it.

Reuben's close friend Rabbi Janet Burden decided to take the funeral service herself even though it would be an ordeal for her. At least she would not get his name wrong as happened at my stepmother's funeral.

A few days passed before the day of the funeral. When we got to the cemetery, nothing was happening. There was no sign of the hearse. The waiting was atrocious but finally the hearse and the absurdly dressed undertakers arrived. Why these paid mourners wear Victorian costumes remains a mystery.

The coffin was brought into the all-purpose chapel and Janet began the service.

Then the final calamity. We walked behind the coffin to the plot which had been prepared. Aileen was sobbing. Nicholas was crying. So was I, but I collected myself to say Kaddish, which I still say every day for Reuben.

DOI: 10.4324/9781003272670-11

So, there it was. My son was in the ground. His mother and brother were weeping. I was weeping. We went to his mother's house and shared memories of him. I can't remember what we said.

It is now time to turn from the personal to what science tells us.

Psychological research

According to several studies, between 65 and 95 per cent of mothers and 51 and 85 per cent of fathers report being preoccupied and having irrational thoughts about their dead baby during the acute phase of grieving. Many parents report a sense of the baby's presence – of hearing their dead baby cry – and some mothers say they feel foetal movements for months after the delivery. Others report illusions or hallucinations that their baby is still alive.

Most research focuses on the loss of a spouse or a parent so what follows is based on fewer studies than one might wish. One 2015 study of 2512 bereaved adults (many of whom were mourning the loss of a child) found little or no evidence of depression in 68 per cent of those surveyed shortly after the tragedy (Maccallum et al., 2015). About 11 per cent initially suffered from depression but then improved; roughly 7 per cent had symptoms of depression before the loss, which continued unabated. For 13 per cent of the bereaved, chronic grief and clinical depression began only after their lives were turned upside-down by the death. It is entirely possible to be deeply sad without being depressed.

Most studies have been clinical descriptions of participants in support groups (like The Compassionate Friends), so the findings are likely to have been influenced by the fact that those individuals chose to seek this type of help and by the participants' experiences in the groups. As a result, the findings cannot be generalised. Researchers have usually only looked at functioning for a brief period during the acute phase of bereavement. Few studies have examined longer-term outcomes, and most that have used retrospective reports that are possibly fallible. Memory of normal events is far from perfect. Of traumatic ones? We do not remember that well how we coped years later (e.g., Nelson and Frantz, 1996; Stehbens and Lascari, 1974).

Stroebe, Stroebe and Abakoumkin (2005) found that bereaved persons, especially those presenting with extreme emotional loneliness and severe depressive symptoms, were at risk of thinking of suicide. Li et al. (2005) found that bereaved parents, especially mothers, were at greater risk than average of being admitted to a psychiatric hospital. The likelihood of mothers being hospitalised remained significantly higher five years or more after the death. Mortality rates were higher among bereaved than non-bereaved parents, particularly for deaths due to unnatural causes (such as accidents and suicide) within the first three years of the child's death (Li et al., 2003). Bereavement was associated with long-term mortality due to illness (e.g., cancer) for the mothers, presumably because of stress, a weakened immune system or the fact that they smoked and drank.

One acid test is how well marriages survive. One study indicated that the divorce rates among bereaved parents are as much as eight times the norm

(Lehman, Wortman and Williams, 1987). A review by Oliver (1999) challenged this conclusion as many limitations associated with sampling and difficulties in tracking divorced couples make it impossible to draw clear conclusions (Murphy et al., 2003).

There is no orthodoxy, but some models propose that grief reactions should be completed within a few weeks to a few months after a death. However, Becvar (2003) suggested that a more typical time line of grief begins with shock and intense grief for two weeks, followed by two months of strong grieving and then a slow recovery that takes about two years. Other studies suggest that even this is too short when a child dies. Murphy et al. (2003) found that parents reported thinking of the death of their child daily three and four years later. McClowry et al. (1995) found that parents whose child died of cancer still experienced pain and a sense of loss 7–9 years later.

There is no more intimate bond than that with your child. If it is ruptured, it is not ruptured. The emotional ties may not be fully severed, and negative emotions might persist despite other forms of positive adaptation (Murphy et al., 2003). Thus, many parents grieve indefinitely (Klass, 1999; Rubin, 1993).

For all the shortcomings of research one finding seems surprising. Most parents seem to manage without significant long-term disruption in major life domains; for others, however, "moving on" does not happen smoothly.

Shane Dunn (2020) pondered

> which stage I was in. I wondered if it was either a circle of grief or a spectrum of grief. Then I decided not to consider it at all. *To hell with that,* I thought. I will find a bar. I will not think.
>
> I will ignore the void.
>
> One car ride later and I was at a bar. A bar where you could smoke to your heart's content, buy boiled eggs, and observe and engage until shutdown at 7 a.m. "How quaint!" I thought as I marvelled at the Old Style signs and ancient photos. "How fitting!" I thought as I watched the derelict night owls fly from bartender to bathroom, jukebox to dance floor. Who could blame me? Me, myself? Why would I blame myself? I am going through a loss; I am suffering as others suffer. If I find myself hovering over a toilet bowl with a hangover and heaving breath, let it come. As long as I find what I seek, the means matter little to me.
>
> I ordered a beer, got a can filled with water for ash. I lit a cigarette, pulled out my sea-green notebook. I armed myself with a pen. I began writing. I filled it one word at a time. Smooth sentences and broken fragments. Precise paragraphs and earthbound ellipses. Serrated quotation marks and dagger dashes. I wrote without care, without conscious thought.
>
> But when I put down the pen and read what I'd scribbled, I saw a pattern.
>
> Everything was a question.
>
> What do you do when you wake up after a wonderful night where your creation juices flowed and mingled with the minds of others, only to check

your phone and see several missed calls, with texts all saying, "please call back, it's really urgent"?

What do you do when your sister has died but you felt it coming many moons ago, intuitively, with reason and yet without?

What do you do when your family is full of tears and sorrow, yet there you stand in stoic solitude?

What do you do when you see your sister carried away in a white plastic body bag on a deep-blue stretcher?

How well parents are and what resources they have before the death affects the extent of disruption and the need for professional help (Kazak and Noll, 2004). Following Frankl, recent work stresses finding meaning in the loss as key to long-term recovery (Neimeyer, 1998). Frankl described the vast emptiness bereaved individuals feel as "existential vacuum" (1978). Grief has also been described as the loss of an "assumptive world." The world is no longer stable, no longer predictable, no longer safe. Parents need to find something to regain a shred of well-being (Klass, 1999).

But what can help? Frankl once told a patient who was dying of cancer to get interested in East Africa. When I interviewed Harold Leopold Loewenthal, an eminent Freudian who also lived in Vienna, he mocked this as ridiculous, but he may have missed the point. Frankl's patient became interested in Africa, and he claimed it took her mind off her coming death. Is studying East Africa silly – yes – but it could be distracting. For children Frankl's ideas are less practical. Imagine the conversation.

"Yes, Amanda, I know you're dying but wouldn't you like to be buried with top marks in a gold star coffin?"

Still there is evidence that the following make the trauma a more bearable experience – doing satisfying work, participating in community and religious organisations (Sherkat and Reed, 1992), having another child after the death and investing in relationships with the remaining children (Najman et al., 1993). Videka-Sherman (1982) considered that having another child after the death was a "constructive action" for the parents and found it predicted better psychological adjustment to the loss. However, having another child might have unexpected costs, as parents with larger families experienced more estrangement, more anger and less openness as they dealt with the loss of a child (Nelson and Frantz, 1996), perhaps because more children overtaxed their resources.

The family background information in the Wisconsin Longitudinal Study (Hauser et al., 1993) gave the Danish team the opportunity to match bereaved mothers and fathers to a comparison group with similar characteristics. They identified enough bereaved parents to detect even small effects for a non-clinical sample that was not self-selected for this purpose.

The specific hypotheses were:

- *Hypothesis 1:* The majority of parents were expected to cope but those who experienced the death of a child would be more likely to report depressive symptoms, poor psychological well-being, health problems, taking less part in social activities, marital disruption and doing less well at work. Yet the researchers also expected bereaved parents would report a greater sense of purpose in life and taking part in more religious activities.

- *Hypothesis 2:* Recovery would be helped by the individual's ability to find a sense of purpose in life, as well as through activities that give life meaning, such as religious participation, social participation, having a satisfying job, having other children at the time of death and giving birth to a new child after the death. They expected these factors would moderate the differences between the bereaved and the comparison parents and would predict better recovery within the bereaved group.

The final group consisted of 144 fathers and 284 mothers. The men were less likely than women to report deaths that occurred during or shortly following childbirth.

(Rogers et al., 2008) examined bereaved parents of deceased children (infancy to age 34) and comparison parents with similar backgrounds (n = 428 per group) identified in the Wisconsin Longitudinal Study. An average of 18.05 years following the death, when parents were age 53, bereaved parents reported more depressive symptoms, poorer well-being and more health problems and were more likely to have experienced a depressive episode and marital disruption than were comparison parents. Recovery from grief was associated with having a sense of purpose in life and having additional children but was unrelated to the cause of death or the amount of time since the death.

Most studies have used the way participants in grief support groups like The Compassionate Friends describe their lives, so the findings are likely to have been influenced both by the self-selection factors that led individuals to seek this help and by the participants' experiences in the support groups. As a result, the findings may well not apply to the broader population of bereaved parents. Researchers have usually only studied the way people are for a brief period after the death. Few studies have examined what happens years ahead and most that have done so have used retrospective reports which make individuals recall what they were like back then (Nelson and Frantz, 1996; Stehbens and Lascari, 1974).

In general, there is a contradiction. Most parents cannot forget and so many grieve forever; there is no time limit but their grieving may not wreck their lives (Klass, 1999; Rubin, 1993).

Some researchers claim that bereaved parents who have problems before their child dies will suffer more and need more professional help. (Kazak and Noll, 2004). Frankl is again relevant as other recent work emphasises the task of finding meaning in the loss as key to long-term recovery (Neimeyer, 1998).

In a way research just backs up common sense. Do interesting work or make the work you do interesting. Take part in community and religious organisations (Sherkat and Reed, 1992). Or have another child and make more of the relationships with the remaining children (Najman et al., 1993).

Again, however, the picture is not simple. Nelson and Frantz (1996) found that parents with larger families felt more estranged, angrier and less open. More children meant the parents needed to do more but we all can hide our problems and so others may not recognise the state we are in. Rando (1993) has suggested the failure of family and friends to recognise the need for continued emotional support makes things worse.

Meaning and resilience

Parents wait, hope, realise their hopes are turning to ash, dust, wait, despair. In *Waiting for Godot* Beckett's tramps wait for Godot to give their lives some meaning. The questions are timeless:

Why am I here?
What am I doing with my life?
Wouldn't it make more sense if I could turn myself into a tree? Or better yet an anvil so I could be hit.

So, if you want to recover, find meaning in your life. Aileen has found that one of the only ways to help is to be useful. She took a course in poetry and therapy and now runs a weekly group for MIND in Birkenhead where people discuss poetry and read their own poems. Aileen's *The Little God of Damage Limitation* won the 2016 Live Canon anthology prize. It is a book for and about Reuben and the loss of Reuben. Theories of grief sometimes speak of recovery. Losing a child is not like having an illness. Aileen has found ways to survive; she stresses *survive*, not recover. Every session she does at MIND, however, has a kickback, as she says, "I can do this, to start with, and then I can help strangers and not my own son". This theme recurs but having no purpose in life is itself a symptom of more general depression, which makes it complicated to untangle one's mental state and the hammer blow of the death of a child.

However, having a purpose in life also predicts better health. It sounds evangelical and rather counter to the principles of some therapies but it is likely that helping bereaved individuals find meaning in the death and develop a renewed sense of purpose might be as useful as ironing out their complexes. Having another child following the death can be regarded as a way of finding meaning (Videka-Sherman, 1982). Other research has reported lower rates of psychiatric problems for bereaved parents with more children in the family (Li et al., 2005). If you have to keep on being a parent, it should make it easier to live on.

The recently developed Two-Track Model of Bereavement may be useful (1999). How people function generally after a death is the topic of Track I. Track II focuses on how people change and maintain their relationships with significant others.

On Track I, the details assessed include:

1 The degree of anxiety and depressive responses and what triggers them
2 Other responses such as guilt and helplessness. (These two emotions are very different. I may feel very guilty but can manage routine tasks and do not imagine my work colleagues are conspiring against me.)

3 Physical problems
4 Psychiatric symptoms including orientation and mental status, PTSD and suicidal thoughts
5 Self-esteem
6 The ability to work or perform normal life tasks, like making sure you pay your rent on time and do not miss important meetings
7 Managing family relationships, including those with a spouse or partner, to other children and to the extended family
8 The nature and degree of involvement in relationships outside the family
9 What other structures is the bereaved involved in and how he or she is different in relation to them? For example, does the bereaved person still go to play darts in the pub? Do they still ride with their bicycling club?
10 The degree to which the bereaved person can invest emotional energy in life tasks and the type of life tasks that are engaged in.

Track II examines nine other, far more introspective dimensions. These include:

1 How preoccupied a person is with memories and thoughts of the deceased
2 The degree to which the dead child is idealised
3 Any report of psychological conflict or contradictions in the relationship
4 The degree and type of positive affect and emotion
5 The degree and type of negative emotion towards the deceased
6 The degree of closeness or distance from the relationship and experience of the deceased
7 The emotions when discussing the deceased (e.g., a parent who might say, "I always feel guilty thinking about how my son died")
8 The presence of previously described grief phases of shock, seeking reminders of the deceased and having to surface through confusion
9 The manner in which the dead are remembered both publicly and within the family.

Time does not heal

The anger grieving parents feel may be directed at a spouse, at other family members, at the professional staff, at God, at fate or even at the dead child. And at surviving children in the family.

All parents have dreams about their children's futures; when a child dies the dreams may die too and the future.

Parents' experiences when a child dies include:

1 The loss of sense of personal competence and power
2 The loss of a part of the self
3 guilt and self-blame (these are especially pronounced following the death of a child – the death makes nonsense of the idea that the parent should look after the child.

Too much hope can be vested in the children who survive.

Parents sometimes say their grief continues all their lives, often saying, "It gets different, it doesn't get better." Words such as "closure" can be deeply offensive. The few studies that have followed parents for years make clear the pain and their preoccupation with the loss of children lasts as long as they live. Klass (1999) invokes the "amputation metaphor": the vivid sense of a permanent loss of a part of oneself to which one can adapt, but it will not grow back. Amputees often feel so-called "phantom limbs." You may have lost your arm but the nerves tingle as if it were still there.

Parents resist what they often feel is the spurious hope that they will recover from their child's death. Rather than "recovery" or "resolution," some speak of "reconciliation" and "reconstitution" because these terms better reflect the profound changes that take place when a child dies. You are never the same.

Aileen is astonished that I appear to be the same. I am and am not. She thinks I am a master of denial, but I think of Reuben every day.

Even the "successful" mourning process changes one. Despite the harrowing accounts reported, some studies show that more than a few bereaved individuals show no overt signs of grieving. They breeze on as if nothing had happened. In *The Importance of Being Earnest,* Lady Bracknell says of a recently widowed society lady that her hair has turned quite gold from grief. That does not happen when a child dies.

The question these findings raise is to what extent such resilience may also be found among those mourning the death of a child. The evidence is not clear. A 2001 study (Lannen et al., 2010), for example, surveyed 449 parents who had lost a child to cancer 4–9 years earlier. While both mothers and fathers healed over time, about 20 per cent still reported unresolved grief a decade after their loss. Mothers were more likely to display low psychological and physical well-being overall. Fathers were more likely to report low quality of life, difficulty sleeping and nightmares.

The researchers asked each parent one simple question: "Do you think that you have worked through your grief?" Four to nine years after the loss of a child, 26 per cent of parents of a sample of 116, said that their grief remained "unresolved," and these parents were followed up. Time did not heal much. Forty per cent of fathers and 35 per cent of mothers reported unresolved grief at year six. But by year seven, that figure dropped to 25 per cent of fathers and 18 per cent of mothers. Unfortunately, at years 8 and 9, there is nothing more than incremental improvement.

Researchers then asked each of the 116 parents with unresolved grief to respond to a battery of tests including the Spielberger State-Trait Anxiety Inventory (Spielberger, 1983) and the Centre for Epidemiologic Studies Depression Scale (Radloff, 1997). About a quarter of parents with unresolved grief reported very low quality of life, and very high levels of anxiety and depression. There were few differences between the sexes, but fathers were at slightly higher risk of depression and low quality of life, while mothers had higher rates of anxiety and low overall psychological health.

Time does not heal – you can never have your child back. But religion does offer some consolation to believers. Augustine of Hippo said in his *Confessions* (2008):

> Of necessity, we must be sorrowful when those whom we love leave us in death. Although we know that they have not left us behind forever, but only gone ahead of us. Still when death seizes our loved ones, our loving hearts are saddened by death itself. Thus the apostle Paul does not tell us not to grieve, but not to grieve like those who are without hope.

Aileen says:

> Tolerance. Everything depends on that and none of us are good at it, especially when the worst happens. Tolerance of our own intolerance, and our partner's. A will to forget things that shouldn't be said, if they are said.
>
> You're both a bit crazy. That's putting it politely; at times you will be nuts. You're way off balance, and you need holding. You need taking care of. But the person you're married to or with, in whatever sense of the word, is also way off. Treat them and yourself like the poor lunatics you are, and try and get a little shift from that. A little nursing of the other when you can manage it will make you feel a little more together yourself. Even a small act or word of kindness can go a long way. Because you are partners in crime. The crime of losing a child, as it feels, is there with you and between you. It's a hard, hard thing to share. But if you can both bear it, if you can share the weight of it, it will open up a little breathing space.

The most famous example of a mother witnessing the death of a child is, of course, in the New Testament. Mary is at the foot of the cross on which her son is being crucified. The scene has inspired artists for centuries – and there have been changes in how it has been represented.

Paintings of "The Lamentation" itself started to be done in the eleventh century, always giving a more prominent position to Mary, who initially holds the body, and later has it across her lap, or sometimes falls back in a state of collapse as Joseph and others hold the body. Northern versions made Mary even more central. The typical position of Christ's body was flat on the ground to begin with, but Mary then has the strength to raise Jesus' upper torso and finally hold it in a near-vertical position or across her lap. Mary Magdalene typically holds Jesus' feet.

Belief in the ascension of Mary into heaven became Catholic doctrine in 1950. Pope Pius XII then declared that Mary "was not subject to the law of remaining in the corruption of the grave, and she did not have to wait until the end of time for the redemption of her body (1950)."

As Mary was – forgive the disrespect of the verb – whisked up to heaven, there were no major bodily relics. Although there was breast milk, tears, hair and nail clippings, her relics were mostly "second order" – garments, rings, veils and shoes.

Without bones to venerate, her devotees make do with visions – at Lourdes, Guadalupe, Fatima and Medjugorje, where she can be invoked to ask God to grant their prayers.

But Mary was more than just a saint. In popular devotion she was a sky goddess always dressed in blue. She was the goddess of the moon and the star of the sea (*stella maris*).

Other religions have their own rituals. Like Hinduism and Sikhism, Buddhists believe in reincarnation and the freeing of the soul. To them, death is a natural part of the cycle of life and the way a Buddhist behaved in this life determines his or her future life, through reincarnation.

For Buddhists, the ultimate goal is to liberate themselves from the cycle of death and rebirth to attain nirvana. To do this, they must rid themselves of basic desires and the shackles of the self to achieve total enlightenment.

Close friends and family should be there at the death and think about the good deeds the dying person has done in the hope it will help them in their next reincarnation. Family and friends can perform good deeds on their behalf.

But how does a baby or a young child rid itself of desires or self?

Judaism

God knows about fatherly love in the Bible. To test Abraham, he tells him to kill his son Isaac. Abraham ties the boy down and then God being a drama queen and a master of suspense relents. Killing a ram would do. With sweet smelling spices, of course.

When a Jew dies, his or her family sit Shiva and "welcome" friends. They talk, remember, mourn. But *Walking Through the Valley of the Shadow: When a Jewish Child Dies* (Schrag, 2003) warns parents, "You are very vulnerable, you have enough problems, and you do not need anyone around you who cannot be genuinely sympathetic."

Certain times of year and particular dates may trigger increased anxiety and unhappiness. Most common are the birthday of the child, his or her death date and holidays that held special significance for him or her or for the family.

Your child's favourite holiday celebration may have been the family gathering for Passover Seder or for Thanksgiving, the Fourth of July barbecue and fireworks or building a *sukkah* together. A seat at the table will be empty now, and there will be one less pair of hands to help with preparations or plan the festivities.

Receiving an invitation to a bar or bat-mitzvah, a wedding or a graduation is tough because a child is completing a life cycle event that your child will never reach. It can be extremely upsetting but your primary consideration should be your own feelings. If you are not up to it, tell the host so. A true friend or compassionate relative will understand. If he or she does not, it is his or her problem.

The power of prayer

Few phrases are more difficult to recite than "*Adonai dayan ha-emet*," the pronouncement the bereaved make at the funeral, affirming that "God is the true (or righteous) judge." This is hard to say or hear when your child is being lowered into the ground. For religious Jews this statement of faith ushers in a period of prayer and reflection that can give comfort to many people.

If you are angry with God, and question how a loving or omnipotent God could arbitrarily deprive you of your beloved child, you might not be open to re-examining your feelings or reinterpreting your concept of God. Yet, some people say: "It's okay to be angry with God; He's big enough to handle it." The sentence could have been spoken by the wonderful fictional priest Don Camillo, who often found himself bargaining with God.

But if we recognise our need to talk about our loss, we might think of prayer as a personal communion with God. The rabbi Schrag (2003) says:

> This is a time to look inside for what the Prophet Elijah called "the still small voice" within you and go with your gut feeling. You may regard this process as "prayer," meditation, introspection, or something else. But regardless of the title, it enables you to look deep inside yourself, it gives you the right to question authority, and it reminds you to invoke your sacred responsibility to yourself to put your own needs first at this time.

Different cultures

In Māori culture, traditional beliefs and Christianity combine. According to Rosenblatt (2001), the ceremony of *tangi* has largely resisted the ravages of colonisation and remains deeply embedded in Māori communities. Children are present at *tangi*, are exposed to *tupapaku* or the deceased, and talk about death. It is not taboo.

The dead play an important role in Māori traditions. They are acknowledged at all gatherings. This remembering of those who have passed away serves to remind Māori of the importance of life, people and relationships.

For the *tangihanga* ceremony the body is usually prepared by an undertaker and displayed in an open coffin. A *tangi* often takes three days and used to be held outside, but with the increase of urbanisation it can be held in a hall or a private home.

The body is welcomed onto the *marae* with the bereaved. Over the course of the *tangihanga* visitors are welcomed onto the *marae* and traditional speeches, songs and chants are exchanged.

The traditional process of exhuming and reinterring bones has been replaced by the ceremony of *hura kōhatu* (unveiling the gravestone), usually a year after the *tangi*.

In a ceremony called *kawe mate* (carry the dead) the memory of a person will be taken to those who were unable to attend the *tangihanga*. The deceased person is represented by a photograph.

When asked about their beliefs about an afterlife, the parents in Rosenblatt's study (2001) explained that they came to know and believe in a Christian afterlife, a Māori afterlife or some combination of both. Rosenblatt argued it was quite common for many traditional societies to blend culture and religion without it being difficult to find comfort and understanding of death from both perspectives.

12 Social media

We are bombarded with information. There is much controversy now about social media and whether social media platforms have any duty of care to users. Now that Elon Musk has become Chief Twit as he puts it, more freedom of speech is likely to produce more trauma for bereaved parents.

Beeban Kidron, a crossbench peer and chair of the 5Rights Foundation, is calling for social media firms to be required by law to hand over data when a child dies.

"The first thing to say is this case is one parent of many," Baroness Kidron said, speaking of Molly Russell.

> I speak to a lot of parents whose children have taken their own lives.
>
> They try to access the material online and they face a block. That block goes on for years. There is no higher authority to appeal the sort of things tech companies tell them and it is absolutely inhuman.
>
> The weight of not knowing is crippling, they can't come to terms with what happened.

Five years ago, Molly Russell's father, Ian, said:

> Molly's feelings of worthlessness grew and her sense of helplessness deepened, as ending her life seemed to her like a solution – while to us her life seemed very normal. It is sadly all too easy to look back and think of the torment Molly must have endured, the pain she must have experienced, and the isolation she must have felt so deeply.

He added:

> It's all too easy to dwell on the events that led Molly to end her life. It's all too easy to forget the person she really was: someone full of love and hope and happiness, a young person full of promise and opportunity and potential. And so, as this inquest starts, we, her family, think it is essential to remember who Molly really was so we can each hold a picture in our

DOI: 10.4324/9781003272670-12

minds of a caring individual, full of love and bubbling with excitement for what should have lay ahead in her life.

Ian Russell read tributes from Molly's friends, including a poem read at her funeral and said:

> Thank you for inspiring us to face our fears, for making us want to do better, for encouraging us to grow and be good people. Thank you for showing us that we can get through the rain . . . and for believing in ourselves.
>
> She was an easy-going young girl. She was happy in her own company. She loved being with her sisters just as they loved being with her. She was always the one who could be relied on to snuggle up to you on the sofa. She was self-supporting and capable.

Yet all that did not stop her taking her own life. Molly tweeted or retweeted 460 times, liked 4100 tweets and used Pinterest, with more than 15,000 engagements. In her last six months she was engaging with Instagram posts about 130 times a day on average.

Ian Russell continued:

> Just as Molly would have wanted, it is important to seek to learn whatever we can and then to take all necessary action to prevent such a young life being wasted again. For everyone touched by her story, remember there's always help and hope. Remember to live long and stay strong as Molly wished.

The inquest had moments of conflict. Covering guilt and greed is always tricky, especially when those involved are corporates.

Elizabeth Lagone, head of health and well-being at Meta, which owns Instagram, told the inquest she believed it was "safe for people to be able to express themselves" online. But the posts were "complex" and often a "cry for help." The last phrase has often been used in research on attempted suicide. O'Brien used it in *The Negative Scream* (1979) and stressed that sometimes the suicide attempt fails but sometimes not.

The inquest was told that out of the 16,300 posts Molly saved, shared or liked on Instagram in the six months before her death, 2100 were related to depression, self-harm or suicide.

When Ms Lagone was shown each post the Russell family's lawyer, Oliver Sanders KC, asked whether she believed they promoted or encouraged suicide or self-harm. She said she thought it "safe for people to be able to express themselves" but conceded two of the posts would have violated Instagram's policies.

Instagram's guidelines at the time said users were allowed to post content about suicide and self-harm to "facilitate the coming together to support" other users but not if it "encouraged or promoted" this.

Ms Lagone said she thought the content Molly Russell saw was "nuanced and complicated," adding that it was important to give people a voice if they were experiencing suicidal thoughts.

Another witness Jud Hoffman, Pinterest's global head of community operations, said he was "not able to answer" how children could agree to potentially being exposed to content inappropriate for a child.

The court saw the platform's terms of service where users were asked to report "bad stuff" if they saw it on the site. The terms of service, from November 2016, warned users might be exposed to material that was "inappropriate to children."

Oliver Sanders KC asked him:

> Bearing in mind it might be children who are opening the account . . . when a user opens an account they have to agree there may be content that's inappropriate for a child. If the user is a child, how can they agree to that?

"I'm sorry, I'm not able to answer that," Hoffman said, and added he deeply regretted that Molly saw content relating to self-harm, suicide and depression on the platform. He was taken through a number of images the company had sent to Molly via email before her death, with headings such as "10 depression pins you might like" and "depression recovery, depressed girl and more pins trending on Pinterest."

The emails also contained images and Mr Sanders asked Hoffman if he believed they were "safe for children to see."

He replied, "So, I want to be careful here because of the guidance that we have seen. I will say that this is the type of content that we wouldn't like anyone spending a lot of time with."

Sanders asked, "Do you think people, particularly children, would find it very difficult . . . to make sense of the content?" to which Mr Hoffman replied, "Yes."

The court then heard how Pinterest used artificial intelligence and human moderators to hide or remove content related to self-harm and suicide, a system that was "largely successful," but users might still encounter such content.

Oliver Sanders suggested Pinterest had "chosen to take a risk" when there was a "no-risk option" of not allowing children on Pinterest.

"I would say 'chosen an option other than absolutely no risk', I would not say 'risky option' . . . obviously our intention is to reduce the risk," Hoffman replied.

The inquest was shown two streams of content Molly had seen on Pinterest. The first included a wide variety of content, but the latter was dark focusing on depression, self-harm and suicide.

Hoffman agreed that the tone of the content had changed and added, "I deeply regret that she was able to access some of the content shown." He agreed the platform was not safe when Molly used it – and admitted harmful content still "likely exists" on the site.

Sanders then asked: "Pinterest accepts that its platform should be safe for children?"

Hoffman replied, "It should be safe for everyone on the platform."

Sanders continued, "And it accepts that in 2017, when Molly was on it, it wasn't safe?"

Hoffman replied, "That's correct, there was content that should have been removed that was not removed." He then qualified his statement by saying, "Content that violates our policies still likely exists on our platform. It's safe but imperfect and we strive every day to make it safer and safer."

Coroner Andrew Walker asked, "It's not as safe as it could be?"

Hoffman replied: "Yes, because it could be perfect."

Molly's father, Ian Russell, appeared on *Good Morning* on November 29, 2022, He said the companies were so rich fines would make no impact and suggested executives should be charged with corporate manslaughter in some cases.

Yet another death has received less publicity

Mariano Janin's 15-year-old daughter, Mia, is believed to have taken her own life on March 12, 2021 after being bullied online and in person. In an interview with *Jewish News*, her father expressed frustration about the way his late daughter's school, Jewish Free School, responded to the tragedy. "No one" at the Kenton-based Jewish secondary school "took accountability for what happened to Mia, and nothing has changed. The same governors were still at the school. It had happened before. If bullies get impunity, they don't learn any lessons."

He added that his wife often said that if her late father, Alexander Neumann, a survivor of several Nazi concentration camps, had heard of the way his granddaughter was bullied at a Jewish school, he "would turn in his grave."

"I just need to have closure to find out what happened. We need to do what we can to avoid this happening again," said Mr Janin.

"Every day now feels like I'm in slow motion," said Mr Janin. Several months after Mia took her own life, Mariano died from an aggressive form of sudden-onset cancer.

"When it happens, you don't see the future, you can't see your past; it's been a painful and slow-motion process. As a parent you're not supposed to bury your kids," Mr Janin said.

Some charities have called for legislation to compel social media companies to hand over data linked to cases where children have taken their own lives. In an open letter, 37 charities called for a clause to be added to the Online Safety Bill currently going through Parliament. Given the political turmoil of autumn 2022 it is not clear if the Bill will survive.

13 Mourning and marriages

Does the tragedy of a death of a child make couples grow closer or drive them further apart?

Most studies have focused on divorce as a sign of stress for the parents, but the evidence is patchy. Bohannon (1991) concluded that some writers exaggerated estimates of divorce. However, he found that about 30 per cent of husbands and wives reported having more negative feelings towards their spouse since the death; 19 per cent of husbands and 14 per cent of wives felt their marriages had deteriorated. About the same proportion had considered divorce after the death, but the frequency of divorce in the US population is about 50 per cent. As a result, separating the "real" contribution of the death of a child from other causes of marital strife is not at all easy.

In 1999 The Compassionate Friends, a self-help organization, completed a survey of 14,852 parents who had lost a child, *When a Child Dies: A Survey of Bereaved Parents*. It found newly bereaved parents frequently feel upset when they read or hear about high divorce rates among couples after the death. However, 72 per cent of parents who were married at the time of their child's death were still married to the same person when the study was done. The remaining 28 per cent included 16 per cent in which one spouse had died, and only 12 per cent of marriages had ended in divorce. The divorce rate among bereaved parents was substantially lower than is often cited.

Most studies are limited by the lack of a control group, selection bias and the fact that subjects drop out. Some studies have found that as many as 25 per cent of couples felt closer in their marriage after the death. As Rando suggests (1996) couples need to be informed that people experience grief differently and be reassured that relationships can and do survive after a child dies.

Four studies focused on features such as marital closeness (Song et al., 2010), marital satisfaction (Wijngaards-de Meij et al., 2007), how interdependent the couple were (Stroebe et al., 2001; Wijngaards-de Meij et al., 2008). Again, researchers have invented terms such as "discordant coping", which may be worse than "incongruent grieving." Jargon is a way of distancing.

Prigerson and Jacobs (2001a) found a tendency in parents to blame the mother for the baby's death (26 per cent of mothers and 13 per cent of fathers), even though doctors explained there was no reason to do that.

DOI: 10.4324/9781003272670-13

Blaming is not easy to avoid in many marriages but after a death it is infinitely more than domestic accusations – you never do the hoovering properly – or physical ones – you never touch me unless you want sex. When a child dies, couples often blame each other, saying:

"It was your fault."

"No, it was yours."

Conflict and anger, at times directly or indirectly blaming the spouse for the death, are frequently described as a way of dealing with the pain.

A descent into silence. Couples avoid all discussion of the death or misunderstandings about it.

I had not heard of "discordant coping'" before writing this book. Research reinforces stereotypes. Women tend to use more emotional expressions as they try to cope, while men try to control their emotions and cope with them alone. Hence discordant.

Another term the literature offers is "incongruent grieving" as fathers and mothers react with different levels of intensity and for different periods of time – women typically grieve more intensely and for longer.

In Tennessee Williams' *Cat on a Hot Tin Roof* (first performed 1955), Big Daddy observes that marriages are made and unmade in bed. After a trauma a couple may have very different needs for sexual intimacy and that hardly makes for any solace. If you feel less close to your partner, it is hardly surprising grief feels more unbearable and lasts longer.

Practical help matters. Helping with domestic chores and childcare, arranging for the spouse to have time to herself and supporting the spouse in work, life and study are obvious. But loss makes demands on fathers to be strong, repressing their own feelings in the presence of family members, putting the spouse's grief before their own.

According to Reilly-Smorawski, Armstrong and Catlin (2002), attending grieving groups helps. Usually, fathers participate less than mothers in such groups. Because of this, arranging peer support and various support groups for fathers who have lost a child is important.

A difficult issue is visiting the grave. I do it at least once a month, checking Reuben's grave is well tended. I place a stone on it and then say the Kaddish. He was buried in his talis, the shawl Jews wear on their bar mitzvah. I don't think of this usually but now I realise it must have frayed by now.

Bereaved parents Field and Berhman (2003) wrote:

> The death of a child completely shatters you. You're the same people, but at the same time, you're really not. Everyone changes throughout the course of a marriage, but it's rarely so sudden and complete. So, you have to get to know each other again in one of the most harrowing circumstances imaginable.

No two people grieve in the same way. One partner might be very vocal about how he or she is feeling, while the other remains very quiet. One might express grief in "traditional" ways (crying, etc.), while the other does things his or her partner finds odd. You're also rarely grieving on the same "cycles," so to speak. Sometimes you resent your partner for bringing you down when you're having a good day. Sometimes, you feel guilty for bringing your partner down.

There are times in grieving when you want to be – *need* to be – selfish. You don't want to consider somebody else's feelings, only your own. You want to be taken care of, and you want to believe what you're going through is the worst and no one can *possibly understand* how much you hurt. But you *do* have someone who understands, and it's both a blessing and a curse. A blessing not to have to walk the path alone. A curse because some days it's all you can do to help *yourself* survive, let alone someone else. Shutting down and shutting out becomes a coping mechanism.

You're also forced to address difficult situations and emotions that you might otherwise be able to ignore. It would be easy to ignore the complicated things if you were grieving solo – you could just say that no one understands and leave it at that. But with a partner in grief, you're really forced to examine painful concepts and memories if you ever want to rebuild your life. Sometimes you have to do that at someone else's pace, and it's frustrating.

In 2017 Heather Spour wrote in the *Huffington Post*:

> I asked my husband Mike why he thought our marriage survived after our daughter Maddie's death, and he paused and then said, "I don't know." I don't either. We didn't love each other more or better than couples whose marriages ended. I think it helped that on the days we couldn't bear to speak to each other, we could write how we were feeling and decide if we wanted the other to read it. In the beginning we realized that the best way to take care of us, the couple, was to take care of us, individually. We allowed each other to be selfish, but we worked on keeping our communication open and honest. When one of us needed more, we tried not to let it fester. We still work on that.
>
> We give each other space when we need it, and we hold each other when we need that.

You cannot call parents who lose a child lucky, but maybe they can be lucky – and wise – with each other.

14 How brothers and sisters react

Freud wrote about his pleasure when his infant brother Julius died. He repressed the memory but it came back to him during his self analysis and then he remembered the deep jealousy he had felt when his brother Julius was born before Freud was two years old. Freud had four sisters but he was not jealous of them. Sibling jealousy is an issue addressed too little in the literature on grief.

Siblings: The Forgotten Grievers (Zelauskas, 1981) reflected the lack of focus in practice and research on grieving brothers and sisters. Over the past two decades, more attention has been given to the subject. Qualitative studies and personal narratives documented how much they suffered and how their grief often affected them all of their lives. It was made worse when people did not realise that.

Nick has had to bear the pain of a brother. I know it is different from mine. You feel guilty you have lost a child, guilty you have made your other child suffer through that. And anxious that Nick can cope with the pain. He worries for me and especially for his mother. And we worry he worries.

Nick has written eloquently about Reuben for this book, which you can read in his tribute at the end.

As ever the problem is that many studies are retrospective. They suggest that sisters and brothers who survive may feel isolated and withdrawn both at home and with peers. They feel different from peers and lose interest in once normal activities. Playing football does not matter any longer. Whether you wear a green or black dress is trifling. Parents and teachers reported siblings were less socially competent and tended to withdraw. Siblings themselves described feeling guilty, anxious and depressed. Parents have noted problems with sleeping, nightmares, anxiety and PTSD symptoms.

Brothers and sisters are not immune from the *whys* and the *if onlys*. Children can feel in some way responsible for the sibling's death just as they sometimes do when parents fight and divorce.

Perhaps there never really was the close relationship between siblings that people sometimes think. One story I was told illustrates how dark it can get. A friend lost her little girl in a playground accident. The daughter and her brother had been playing together, and he had egged her on to climb to a height she couldn't manage. She fell and died of multiple injuries.

DOI: 10.4324/9781003272670-14

The mother was devastated, full of pent-up anger towards her son. For some weeks she was unable to forgive him. She confided to my colleague that she was struggling with resentment towards the boy. In her heart she wondered why he hadn't been the one to die rather than her daughter.

About six months after the accident, someone talked to both her and the boy about his sister's death. At first, he said nothing at all. Then suddenly he looked up, his face drawn and chiselled in misery, and said, "I killed her." He had not, of course, but he knew his mother blamed him.

Human beings have been described as the only species that talks and the only species that laughs. Neither is quite true but maybe we should also be described as the only species that blames.

Freud on the Web

One can only imagine what Freud would have posted on his website if there had been the internet in his day. Psychologists are only human and like evidence which confirms their ideas so Freud would, I think, be pleased at the fact that siblings who feel guilty post confessions about why they hate their brothers and sisters. It is no accident that David Suchet has played both Freud and Poirot as the two men have some similarities. Poirot often observes there is every difference between wanting someone dead and ladling cyanide into their tea. There is no way of knowing how typical or honest those I quote are, but they reflect a mood at least. One Webber said:

> Morally, you have every right to despise, hate, and otherwise have unpleasant feelings toward your sister—that is, if she's done something truly wrong to you. What has she done to make you feel this way?

Sally Maria Renata posted:

> It depends on whether you wish her gone because of who she is, or whether it's because she displaced your position in the family. In the latter case, it isn't personal, and it has more to do with how your parents are treating you. If this is the case, it's so important to try to communicate your feelings to your parents. They may not understand, they may not be able to change, but at least you come to terms with what the problem is, and you are doing all you can do to fix it.
>
> If it is personal, and it's because your sister's actions infringe on your rights, reflects on your reputation.

Another Webber admitted:

> I hate my sister who died before I was born. What can I do about it?

She got an answer.

I'm going to go out on a limb here and assume you feel resentful towards the emotions and attention your parents give her memory.

It's actually perfectly natural and normal of you to feel this way.

Notice I did not say good.

It is good that you seem to recognize it isn't good and want to stop, however.

Understand that the way we are built as humans for survival we have to feel competitive. We rely on our parents to care for us when we are young and if we do not feel some desire to fight for attention, we may not get it and will not thrive.

Another asked:

Is it wrong to feel like you hate your sibling?

There was one comforting answer.

No, it's completely right if you hate your sibling, you see even I have a sister and everyday I feel like I want to kill her, but I haven't and that's when I realized that I am a better person and I don't want to seek at her level. Nobody understands my pain because according to them I am being ridiculous but I don't give a shit about those people because my sister is the reason why I went into depression and everyday I felt like a failure and my life is going to be destroyed and that's when I realized that it is better to ignore that piece of crap and focus on my own life.

Tests

Complicated bereavement has been less clearly defined for children than adults but is also thought to include symptoms of PTSD, other psychological characteristics associated with this disorder and grief. And psychologists have not failed to forge tests to winkle out its issues. The Expanded Grief Screening Inventory, for example, is a 20-item reviewed by Prigerson et al. Three independent factors govern the scores: positive reminiscing, PTSD on the grieving process and existential loss.

We need to speak what is often unspoken, often unbearable, psychologists argue. Davies (2006) summed up these themes from the sibling's perspective:

1   "I hurt inside" requires comfort, consolation and validation of the child's unique experience of the loss. This is a particularly challenging task for grieving parents.
2   "I don't understand" needs explanation and interpretation provided at a level appropriate to the child's cognitive developmental level. Concerns about the child's own safety and well-being should not be overlooked.

3 "I don't belong" is serious and can be helped by involving brothers and sisters before the death occurs in the case of anticipated loss, during the death and burial rituals.
4 "I'm not enough" requires continual reassurance and validation of the unique worth of each child. This response is somewhat unique to sibling loss compared to other types of losses and has at times powerfully affected how siblings react.

When a child dies, siblings often have to support parents which takes energy and saps emotional reserves, making it harder to care for themselves. One may question if you have the "right" to mourn as deeply as they do, or as a surviving spouse or children do.

Siblings describe a lack of communication and less availability and support from parents. Some have suggested bereaved parents may also become closer to the child or children who survive and overprotective.

Davies (2006) offers guidelines for interventions with bereaved siblings.

1 Children should be helped to feel grief is normal. Recognition of their unique relationship to the sibling and their individual responses to the loss of that relationship should be at the core of any interventions.
2 Siblings are likely to benefit from being included in discussions as early as possible if it is clear their brother or sister is likely to die. Having time allows a brother or sister to begin to absorb the situation and gives an opportunity to provide information, education, emotional support which can make it easier to cope.

Death makes for fear. Children are more likely to fear their own vulnerability to the illness, injuries or condition their sibling suffered. Will I get cancer? The connections are obvious but bleak. Think of them as a chain – mother–father–dead child–living child.

The way parents manage their own grief and try to make sense of their loss has a huge impact on the surviving children. The degree to which parents blame the surviving children, are able or unable to re-establish a positive relationship with them is critical. They need to speak what is often unspoken to begin to cope.

Children complain of a loss of affection, attention, continuity and stability because their parents are preoccupied with their own bereavement. Parents give priority to the dying child. They can think they will be able to make up later to the one or ones who survive.

Friends may not understand or even care. A student bitterly reported a teacher's question, "Why are you upset, he was only your step-brother?" "But he lived with me all my life," she said to herself. Siblings experience a high level of social constraint in response to their grief.

A child may not feel good enough to fill the void in the parents' affection. Parents' intense preoccupation with the dead child is interpreted as a lack of love for the surviving sibling – "the wrong child died." The sibling feels devalued, alienated and isolated from both family and peers.

Suggested approaches include:

> Giving information in multiple formats (e.g., written, audio/visual, internet based, group meeting and larger event) for children and adolescents about the nature of grief following the death of a sibling and ways to cope with it
>
> Giving information about ways to help bereaved siblings to parents, extended family, teachers, coaches, religious and social service organisations, hospitals and health care services, emergency services, mental health providers and the media. Information should include the emerging knowledge about the intertwining of trauma and grief, ways to recognise these symptoms and ways to manage them
>
> Providing opportunities to receive mementos of the child who died and to participate in memorial services
>
> Providing access for bereaved siblings to other bereaved children or adolescents who can share their experiences and reduce isolation. Since sibling death is infrequent, where possible, integrate children and adolescents who have experienced sibling death into existing bereavement groups and services that include children who have experienced loss from the death of a parent or peer or through divorce
>
> Increase knowledge of and provide for the special needs of particular sub-groups of bereaved siblings: those whose sibling died of homicide, suicide, accident or terrorist attack.

Families often avoid both formal and informal support services which is understandable. They want and need to avoid traumatic reminders. However, that may also reflect inappropriate treatment models. An example was reported by the William Wendt Center in Washington, DC, a programme developed to provide trauma and bereavement services to families when they had to identify the body of a loved one who died suddenly from an accident, homicide or suicide. This innovative service worked out of the coroner's office where providers can immediately meet with families upon identification of the body. The center soon discovered that case management services were needed to help families with the consequences of such losses as loss of housing, dramatic loss of income, unsafe living environments and the loss of support networks. Longer-term follow-up of families affected by such traumatic deaths remains a challenge (*Washington Post*, 2013).

15 How fathers react to a child's death

I have described the agony of mothers at many points. Fathers suffer too. In the past men were supposed to be strong and silent. They may have underreported a child's death as a way of coping with grief. If you don't speak about it, it has not happened. I have been accused of being a master of denial myself.

For Freud, denial was a defence against external realities that threatened the ego, and many psychologists would argue that it can be a protective defence in the face of unbearable news. Today to say someone is "in denial" is to deliver a savage combination punch: one shot to the belly for the cheating or drinking or bad behaviour, and another slap to the head for the cowardly self-deception of pretending it's not a problem.

Yet recent studies from fields as diverse as psychology and anthropology suggest that the ability to look the other way, while being potentially destructive, can also help in close relationships. The psychological tricks that people use to ignore a festering problem in their own families can be the same ones that they need to live with everyday human dishonesty and betrayal. Ironically these highly evolved abilities, research suggests, also provide the foundation for forgiveness.

In this emerging view, social scientists see denial on a broader spectrum – from benign inattention to passive acknowledgement to full-blown, wilful blindness – on the part of couples, social groups and organisations, as well as individuals. Seeing denial in this way, some scientists argue, helps clarify when it is wise to use it to manage a difficult person or personal situation, and when it threatens to become a kind of curtain that prevents real contact.

"The closer you look, the more clearly you see that denial is part of the uneasy bargain we strike to be social creatures," according to Michael McCullough, a psychologist at the University of Miami and the author of *Beyond Revenge: The Evolution of the Forgiveness Instinct* (2008).

> We really do want to be moral people, but the fact is that we cut corners to get individual advantage, and we rely on the room that denial gives us to get by, to wiggle out of speeding tickets, and to forgive others for doing the same.

DOI: 10.4324/9781003272670-15

The capacity for denial appears to have evolved in part to offset our ancestors' hypersensitivity to violations of trust. In small kin groups, identifying liars and cheats mattered. A few bad rumours could mean the Neanderthal toad was thrown out of the cave and might be eaten by a passing lion.

One strategy, which may well be unconscious, is simply neglecting to acknowledge the death as real as well as suppressing thoughts about the child or refusing to acknowledge the bereavement. Men do tend to under-report other stressful parenting experiences, like raising a child who has a disability or severe mental illness (Seltzer et al., 2001).

Alcohol

A study by Dawson and his colleagues (2008) carried out on a sample of 26,946 persons, showed a clear association between the number of stressors in the previous year and heavy drinking. It seems plausible that fathers suffer depression and anxiety – and drink.

Pilling et al. (2012) analysed the long-term (three years) effects of bereavement and examined the amount of alcohol consumed, frequency of drinking, alcohol dependence and harmful effects of alcohol use. This Hungarian study relied on self-rating, so the responses may not be altogether objective. The researchers warned mothers might have fudged tests where subjects had to estimate how much they drank and might have tried to hide their alcohol-related problems.

Individuals with alcohol-related problems are often reluctant to seek face-to-face professional help. In one study (Mills-Koonce et al., 2011), fathers had even higher cortisol levels than mothers, which was accounted for by their self-reported increased alcohol intake, which suggested vulnerability to stress.

Many traumatic events like divorce sometimes have benefits. You can feel liberated. To put it crudely a man may think "I've finally got rid of my better half so called and can flit like a butterfly and play the filly field," while a woman may think "'I was so bored with him, his drinking and the way he wanted to shag me while watching darts on the telly."

When a child dies there are no such compensations. The best you can hope for is seeing that your child is out of pain.

The reactions fathers may feel include:

> *Isolation* – in the family and in the world. Kevin Wells told me people crossed the street to avoid talking to him after Holly died. Whenever he challenged them, they said they did not know what to say. Easier for them, harder for him and his family. Some fathers also felt that though close friends and relatives tried to help they failed. It was a Catch 22 situation; help could be irritating but the disappearance of some friends was initially annoying, hurtful and not helpful.
>
> *Depression* – which is made worse by guilt. What did I do wrong? I thought often about how I failed Reuben.

Physical symptoms – these are common. Fathers often reported shivering. Many also sleep badly and have nightmares. I fell down a long flight of stairs soon after Reuben died.

The Ten Commandments tell us to honour thy father and mother but there is no commandment to honour your children. One should not read too much into that, but many fathers feel not just a pervading sense of loss but find themselves asking, "What is the point of life?"

Fathers often did not feel it was necessary to talk as much as mothers did, but silence did not usually mean "closure." You never get over the death of your own child. It is always in your mind because the dead child reminds you of his or her existence every time you look at your other children. Fathers felt that it was useful to get concrete help in the care of their other children, with the funeral arrangements and the hard-to-live times that followed.

There are contradictions again. Samuelsson et al. (2001) reported that fathers badly need to be alone after the death of a child, but at the same time, they need help and support. Some felt a permanent need to withdraw from even the closest relationships. If there were only a few opportunities to participate in the care and decision-making or conflicts over the treatment of the child, that made it harder for fathers to cope with grief.

Fathers felt it was important to be present at the death and experience support for closeness with the dead child, to say goodbye several times, to find out exactly what happened, to get reassurance about what was done and the decisions that were taken.

The support of the obstetrics staff and the hospital chaplain matters (Samuelsson, Rådestad and Segesten, 2001). Some fathers got emotional support from them and the sympathy they provided. It was a comfort when staff expressed their own feelings as well as talking to them professionally. One father said:

> It helped me to cope with regard to my son that they really tried so that it would go well. And that the ITU nurse and the doctor in tears told me all the things and that was something which also helped me to get over it.

However, fathers often felt such support to be too short, inadequate and evasive (de Montigny and Dumas, 1999; McCreight, 2004). What fathers saw as positive support was sad and resigned – a peaceful atmosphere for the child's and parents' last moments together.

Peers gave the most useful support which included grieving together and being together, sharing one's own feelings, talking about experiences and listening and obtaining information on ways of coping. One father said:

> [I]t worked better than I had expected so that it gave me a lot of support. It was somehow easy to identify with them. Everybody knew, and you knew yourself who you were talking to; they had had the same experiences and were sure to understand and what sort of feelings stir in your

mind. It was more like telling, that the people tell, and you get to tell about it and those who had a similar situation, it helped like.

Lack of social support has been linked to complicated and chronic grief (Hazzard, Weston and Gutterres, 1992; Malacrida, 1992). Fathers who had less social support experienced more severe self-reported grief (Zeanah and Boris, 2000). Physicians, nurses and clergy helped in the crisis and immediate post-crisis period (de Montigny and Dumas, 1999; DiMarco, Menke and McNamara, 2001; Hughes and Page-Lieberman, 1989). However, relationships with friends change and can even end completely. There may be so many problems people have no idea what to do with the result that any support may feel and be superficial.

Good employers can help. Research suggests giving fathers' sick leave helps as does accepting diminished efficiency on the job, and sometimes changing a man's job description after the death of the child is helpful.

Close relatives and friends all too often expect men to be strong and finish their grieving process quickly (Worth, 1997), which puts real pressure on sensitive fathers.

Inevitably much research involves questionnaires including the Spielberger State-Trait Anxiety Inventory (Spielberger, 1983).

In *Still Standing* magazine Elizabeth Yassenoff presents an almost romantic picture of the bereaved father as a tragic hero with the headline – "The *Bravest* Dads."

We talk a lot about what bereaved mothers go through and how fierce they are as mothers. But the dads undoubtedly deserve more recognition than they get.

The bereaved dads I know are truly incredible. They help the bereaved mothers pick up the pieces of a life ravaged by grief, while simultaneously grieving themselves.

They put on strong faces as they tell loved ones the news their partner may not be able to utter.

They go before her, preparing the way for her to cautiously re-enter social environments, setting expectations and cautioning others of what she can and cannot handle.

They break down and get vulnerable with her when she needs to know she's not the only one grieving.

They give her space to grieve harder because it was *her* body that carried this child.

Bereaved dads generally have to return to work sooner than mothers. They take refuge in compartmentalisation so they can manage their jobs during the day and do the work of grieving when it feels safe to go there.

They field endless questions of "How is your wife/partner doing?" for months after the loss, and answer them graciously despite the nagging voice in their heads saying, "What about me?"

Perhaps even more than mothers, fathers feel the pressure to "get over it."

That feels a little optimistic. Fathers have not carried the baby, not had that moment-to-moment intimacy. That needs to be taken into account.

16 What can help?

I venture to adapt a famous saying, "We are born alone, we live alone, we die alone but we do not have to let a child die alone."

In 1802, when Napoleon ruled France, the first hospital for children was opened in Paris, the *Hôpital des Enfants Malade*. Germany, Italy, Poland, Austria, Russia and England then opened similar children's hospitals. Once again in Paris, in 1893, Madame Henry, midwife-in-chief of the Port Royale programme for sick babies, recognised they needed special care and set up units called *pouponnières* to provide this facility. She was working at the same time as the great psychiatrist Jean Marie Charcot was showing hysterical patients to his students. Some were women who had lost a child.

In the 1960s Cicely Saunders and Elisabeth Kubler-Ross, both psychiatrists, advocated setting up hospices, first for adults and then for children. The movement began to develop in both the UK and the US.

Nearly 60 years on Cooley and colleagues (2000) showed how little research there still is in paediatric palliative care in general and children's hospices in particular. They looked back to two research projects that tried to evaluate children's hospice care. The first was carried out in the 1980s and had three parts. The first part was a retrospective study of the perceptions of 25 families attending Helen House, Oxford of the care they were receiving. The second compared the experiences of families referred to Helen House but before they had received any care with families who had no intention of asking for a referral. The final part looked at the stresses and job satisfaction of Helen House staff.

The second study was that of Carol Robinson and Pat Jackson (1999) who visited four children's hospices, interviewed families and staff and carried out observations over three days. They found that parents using Helen House services were more satisfied with the support they received than those using the statutory services. The second project's report was also largely encouraging about the quality of services offered.

Dunbar (2006) argued that many parents are relieved to find a place where they feel at "home" and that made the decision to accept help in caring for their child more acceptable.

The Early Days study – conducted by researchers at the University of York's Martin House Research Centre (University of York, n.d.) – also explored

DOI: 10.4324/9781003272670-16

parents' experiences of hospice care in depth. The study interviewed 30 bereaved mothers and fathers from around the UK. Parents varied in how much time they spent with their child, but all found it comforting that they could visit their baby or child at any time and that they remained in a home-like environment.

One parent said:

> It helped me considerably because I was able to go in and just be . . . to hold him, to be near to him, to speak to him, to caress him, to look at him. Because it just allowed us to let go, to say goodbye.

Parents believed that having unrushed time to say "goodbye" had softened their anguish: "It was like an airbag: it cushioned the blow." Another reflected: "It gave us time, knowing he's gone but you've still got longer, which was everything."

An important factor is that many hospices provide "cooling facilities" (e.g., cooled "bedrooms," portable "cooling" cots or blankets), which may have a longer-term, positive impact. It has been suggested cooling gives parents time to spend longer with the body of their child and helps them to accept the reality of their loss and prepare for the changes that will bring to their lives. As one parent put it: "We have something positive to reflect upon following something so harsh."

The origins of cooling can be traced back 40 years to when the UK's first children's hospice, which opened in 1982, included a "cold bedroom" facility. This was subsequently adopted by the 50 or so UK children's hospices set up since then, the majority of which include in-patient/residential services. The recent emergence of portable, electric-powered "cooling blankets/mattresses/cots" has, if offered, opened up to families the option to take their child home rather than staying at the hospice.

Two studies report staff's attitudes and experiences of caring for children using cooling facilities. The first was in a children's hospice (Hackett and Beresford, 2021), the second was based in a hospital in Sweden (Henley et al., 2021) and explored midwives' experiences of using a cold cot. Both explored staff's experiences and reported difficulties managing odour and physical deterioration, and the emotional impact on staff.

Who needs professionals?

Most bereaved people cope without professional help, and over time, will begin to feel better (Kersting et al., 2011; Zisook and Lyons, 1989). But not all parents do recover, so it is important to look at why some intervention programmes work – and some do not. Trying to intervene too early is often well intentioned but not effective. According to Bonanno (2001) and Schut et al. (2001), when you lose a child you feel powerless so it is not surprising that when the bereaved instigates an intervention it tends to work best (Schut et al., 2001). Paradoxically it is surprising that some work suggests the greater distress parents feel correlates with better results (cf. Prigerson and Jacobs, 2001a; Shear, 2015; Zisook et al., 1989; Schut et al., 2001).

Where participants were screened for risk factors, the higher the risk the better the results for those at higher risk (Burke and Neimeyer, 2013; Shear, 2015). Several recent trials of psychotherapy for complicated grief yield moderate to strong effects (e.g., Eisma et al., 2013; Doering and Eisma, 2016). Although these studies identify which interventions work best there are limitations to many of them. Most only assess short-term effects though there are exceptions like Doering and Eisma (2016).

Darian Leader (2009) noted that cognitive behaviour therapy has become fashionable. He writes: "The interesting thing is that now some psychoanalytic therapists are trying to repackage their own work as a version of CBT (Cognitive Behaviour Therapy)." This new psychoanalysis dispenses in practice with the unconscious, infantile sexuality, etc. These new therapies radically change the philosophical underpinning of clinical work – they see human beliefs not as the expression of some inner truth, but as scientific hypotheses about reality. So you can now tell someone seeking a particular form of therapy that they are wrong, that it won't help them.

Eleven studies of CBT found significant benefits were found with CBT-based therapies compared with non-CBT intervention groups for the five domains of grief, depression, anxiety, trauma and general distress at post-treatment, but by the end of the follow-up period the differences between groups remained significant only for depression and anxiety.

"CBT is of course helpful to many people, but for reasons which cannot be subsumed in the cognitive model," Leader (2009) wrote. In the last ten years it has expanded exponentially. He added:

> if you work in the NHS and are using a form of psychotherapeutic or psychoanalytic therapy, drawing on say family systems or psychodynamic work, management are telling you, 'Don't do that, you can't do that, you need to focus on the management of the patients' symptoms.' The overwhelming stance is that these therapies don't work because they are not 'evidence-based'. Thus, the criteria for the evaluation of therapies has moved to a very narrow view of evidence, based on the medical model of randomised-controlled trials. This is the medical model of a trial experiment, with a control group, and so on. You can't do that with therapy, because the whole point of therapy involves the beliefs the person has initially about their treatment or therapeutic experience. So, you can't randomly assign someone to a therapist.
>
> The second point is that, regardless of the tradition being used – whether it's Lacanian, Freudian, whatever – the work is done by the person in therapy, not really by the therapist. The therapist facilitates, but the patient makes the choices.

The current CBT model is basically seen as business. Included in the 450 rules for the conduct of psychoanalysis is something called "skills for business."

It's all based on a business model and a business ethic – you are providing a service to users, they need to be kept happy, you avoid risk, all the things which are pretty incompatible with psychoanalysis. Politically, cognitive behavioural therapies are forcing out other traditional forms of very valid work in this country, which is a serious problem. This ideology is infiltrating the training of other non-cognitive approaches, so training will be pushed further and further into the cognitive model, where there's no place for the unconscious, no place for human history, no place for the dignity of human beliefs.

People who received bereavement counselling saw a greater decrease in grief symptoms over time than those who did not receive counselling. Time itself affected levels of grief in both conditions between baseline and a 12-month follow-up. In the intervention group, grief symptom levels continued to decline; however, between the 12-months and the 18-month follow-up – after counselling had been completed – the control group's mean symptom levels remained unchanged. Those who receive counselling experience a reduction in complicated grief symptoms in addition to the effect of time after the counselling has been completed.

More clinical improvement was observed in complicated grief symptom levels among those who had received counselling intervention; however, this effect was only marginally significant.

The reduction in symptom levels in the control condition approximately matched that of the intervention condition between the baseline and the 12-month follow-up. Were it not for the second factor contributing to the study's results – the substantial drop in complicated grief symptoms after counselling in the intervention group relative to the control group – it might have looked as if the intervention had no effect at all.

One explanation for this delayed effect may be the experience of grief counselling itself. The effort of "working through," which is so much part of counselling, is initially reflected in elevated grief scores, then by a decline after counselling has helped.

The fact that greater symptom change was observed in the intervention group at the 18-month follow-up shows that counselling helps more than the passage of time alone. People may at first attribute feeling better to counselling, whereas time alone might have reduced their suffering as much; but in the long term, counselling does work. The results show the importance of a longitudinal study design, including a long period between measurements. Data collection at additional time points both during and after counselling could also provide more insight into when changes in grief levels occur over time.

The effectiveness of community-based counselling also suggests that it is a potentially cost-effective alternative to professional grief counselling. Though the effect is modest, community-based counselling initiatives currently have a larger reach than professional grief counselling interventions. The sample was predominantly female, as is common (Stroebe and Schut, 2001). In addition, the majority of the sample was bereaved of a parent or partner. Though research has indicated that both the relationship to the deceased person and being a woman increased the likelihood of developing a complicated grief reaction (Burke and Neimeyer, 2013), men have also been shown to be at greater risk of experiencing difficulties specifically after losing their wife (Stroebe, 1998). Further investigation of the effectiveness of bereavement counselling for men and with greater differentiation among bereaved's kinship ties to the deceased would be advantageous. Lastly, excluding participants who take anti-depressant or anti-anxiety medication would have been preferable; however, this was not feasible, given the indications that one in seven Scottish residents take anti-depressants (cf. The Scottish Government, 2014). No differences were found in the use of these types of medications, however, and it is difficult to assess whether prescription drugs had an impact on participants' complicated grief symptoms, indications from a recent large-scale trial by Shear et al. (2016) demonstrating a lack of efficacy of anti-depressant medication alone on complicated grief symptoms make it unlikely that using medication would have influenced outcomes.

The investigation recommended: waiting a number of months post bereavement before providing counselling; offering counselling on an in-reaching basis; incorporating an intake assessment process to screen for complicated grief symptoms and risk factors; and offering a tailored model of counselling. The effectiveness of this approach provides encouragement for supporting community-based initiatives to promote psychological well-being. The counselling service in this investigation was delivered by trained, professional-grade volunteers at a non-profit organisation, where services are available to clients at no cost to themselves. Taken on a broader perspective, considering the long-term effects of elevated grief symptoms (e.g., increased days in hospital) and costs of acute care (cf. Stephen et al., 2015), there are good reasons to conclude that community-based bereavement counselling may allow health boards to increase the availability of support, reduce costs and save rather than spend.

Aileen says she reads aloud to Reuben in his room. "I have done it since he died and hope I can go on doing so until I die". It makes her feel connected to him. "I choose books I know he would love – Murakami, lately a Josh Cohen, and presently *The Books of Jacob* by Olga Tokarczuk, which he would eat up."

There is some element of denial in this, undeniably. And people might find it weird. I think he'd get it. More than denial, I still feel disbelief. And I do not visit the cemetery. I visit his room, and the house is where he most is for me. As many current writers on bereavement now conclude, you bring them with you, or at least you try to. I suppose this book is David's way of trying to do that, and as such I hope it helps him, Nick, and perhaps some other people out there whose names we will never know.

17 Reuben – half a life

We have kept Reuben's room as it was at the top of Aileen's house. We remarried and hoped that would give Reuben some stability. Aileen, Nick and I all have many personal ways of remembering him – if only we didn't need such rituals. On one wall there is a placard saying "Good planets are hard to find." For years the smell of the cigarettes he smoked lingered. We have left some of his clothes in place – two black leather jackets which I sometimes smell for a last taste of him. The smart grey jacket he wore to interviews hangs on a chair. Aileen sometimes sits in an armchair and reads books he would have liked. His computer is still on the desk. And an Israeli ten shekel note. Have we made it a shrine? Yes, anything to keep his memory alive.

How do you sum up what Reuben was and what he might have become? In the Bible three score years and ten – or 70 – is the span of a life. Reuben managed half of that. If he had lived, I am sure he would have written even better books – especially if publishing his books gave him more confidence.

He would, I think, have found a partner who lasted. He was very affectionate except when drugs made him withdraw. I would have been ecstatic if he had had children, but he often said he did not want to. Would coming off drugs have changed that? Death is final and leaves us with questions.

Following Leopold Bloom his headstone should read:

Writer, talker, drinker, smoker, wise beyond his years.

I wish I had called the book *A Book For Reuben* but that only reminds me he is not here to read it.

DOI: 10.4324/9781003272670-17

Extract from *Theo's Ruins* by Reuben Cohen (unpublished)

The old man looks exactly like Freud. Facially, that is; below the neck, where Sigmund was skinny as a prophet in the wilderness, Dr. Theodore Weissman is portly and full. Reclining in his chair, he faces you across the desk, his belly as prominent as the owlish countenance, the old-world reading glasses that adorn his massive head. Thankfully, at least there's no cigar, but the bottomless brown eyes are familiar from a thousand grainy photographs, the pre-war records of the master's face. His gaze, too, is utterly inscrutable; you can almost hear this onetime-therapist withholding.

His flat is of an earlier age, the space in which you sit his consulting room and office. His profession – though you're not sure whether he still takes patients – is symbolised by the couch, a black chaise longue with feet of wooden claw.

He's said nothing for almost a minute, while you counted seconds in your head. Suddenly he breaks the silence.

'Why did you leave Oxford?' he asks.

You notice that the nondescript tie - possibly a relic of some college sojourn of his own – is liberally bedecked with ancient meals. Truly an absent-minded professor.

'It wasn't what I'd hoped for.' Understatement of the century.

'In what way?'

'I arrived with the expectation – naïve in the extreme – of mentorship. And camaraderie. The faculty were perfunctory towards undergraduates, totally uninterested. The last thing I'd expected was to go to Oxford and have no intellectual stimulation.' You pause, watch for a response. His eyes tell you nothing. Nervously, you carry on. 'The company was stuffy and pompous – my college had a male to female ratio of ten to one. You can imagine what that did for the atmosphere. It was like a locker room.' This statement is one you've rehearsed for hours. All of it is true, and reasons you've given are sufficient for departure. They were not, however, the reasons you left.

'I see,' he rumbles, both index fingers at rest now, meeting at the tip of his impressive nose. Deftly, he inserts one into his left nostril and proceeds to full penetration.

DOI: 10.4324/9781003272670-18

It's amazingly easy to ignore such repulsive behaviour. You need him to employ you.

'They assure me your work was satisfactory. Not bad, in fact.'

You didn't know he'd talked to the college. Who on the faculty would be acquainted with so odd a bird as this, with his aura of obscurity and analyst's couch? His glance has acquired a new significance. He's sure to know you're leaving something out. Could anyone have told him? Would he care?

'My grades were ok,' you say after a pregnant pause. 'I just couldn't take the tedium, started to get headaches, migraines, in the hours before class. I wanted to study European thought, the background to psychoanalysis. That would have been impossible til my final year. There didn't seem much point in waiting.'

A Brother's Tribute by Nick Cohen

Sometimes, when the pressure is on, I talk to my brother Reuben. Knowing I was going to have to write something about him, about our relationship, and wanting so desperately to get it right, I hear his voice say, "Nick, it'll be OK. Nothing's perfect. Not even you." He knew how to mock me. He knew my pretensions well. Like any younger brother, who had to grow up in the shadow of someone older and bigger, he knew how to fight dirty. He was a fighter, from the start. Even with the four-year age gap, so huge when we were small, he made up for his size with determination and rage.

Fast forward, and by the time we were teenagers, he was getting bigger, stronger and broader than I was. We shared a teen religion – karate. Every Saturday morning, we made our pilgrimage to Jubilee Hall in Covent Garden and pounded, kicked and sweated our way right up to brown belts. He used those skills on the streets, fighting off muggers at Lewisham station and swaggering into a BNP pub, flashing his star of David pendant and daring anyone to take him on. When a girlfriend of mine cheated on me, he looked up the handsome beau who'd snatched her on social media. "He's not that big," he reported, "I think I could take him."

He fought in so many ways. He fought for truth in our family whenever there were secrets, lies and intrigues, often blurting them out publicly at the dinner table or at Christmases. He fought for his writing, re-working, revising, getting up before dawn. In his publishing work, firstly as a book publicist, championing literary works that faced an uphill struggle to reach readers, latterly running the small press with my Dad where again, he fought against the odds to get unknown authors in front of readers.

He fought and lost his struggle with drugs. He was tapering off benzos, which many medics believe are one of the hardest pharmaceutical addictions, when he relapsed, smoked heroin and died. Even though he lost his own war, he battled to save other addicts, writing passionate and eloquent posts on "Bluelight", an anonymous drug forum, trying to dissuade others from following his path.

When Reuben died, like my parents I was overwhelmed with guilt. I'm the older brother. It is my job to protect. I'd failed spectacularly. I desperately

DOI: 10.4324/9781003272670-19

needed to atone, to cauterise my bleeding wounds. I set about trying to help other young men who I knew or suspected had mental health or drug issues. There was a lad I knew with behavioural issues who had been arrested and was violent. I hired him to help renovate my wreck of a house and made time to try to help stabilise him. One day he was running late to meet me and rang me saying he was about to beat up the cab driver who wouldn't take him because he only had a fifty-pound note. I barely managed to talk him down. I realised that I could not foster a dependency with him that could lead to dangerous places. I'd also been trying to mentor and support another young man, who I could tell was falling into drugs. I talked to his friends about what to do. He found out about these conversations and abruptly broke all contact.

There were other instances, over these years, where I would try to rescue someone who reminds me of Reuben, always to find my efforts went awry. These interventions backfired because I was too desperate. There was too much compensation involved in this rescuing behaviour. They were useful experiences though, in that they brought home the lesson that helping people with mental health and addiction issues can only really be done by professionals. A high level of detachment is essential. I spent many years after my brother's death writing and re-writing a memoir which used his brilliant short stories and unpublished memoirs and counterpointed them with memories and stories of my own. But this unique format was demanding and even though the same literary luminaries who had loved Reuben's work – Andrew O'Hagan and Max Porter – thought it showed immense promise – it remained in Porter's words 'A Cabinet of Curiosities,' which would be difficult for publishers to market.

Ten years on, I've finally paused my work on the memoir and stopped trying to be a surrogate big brother to young men who recall Reuben for me. As I did so, I vividly remembered Reuben, not long before his death, encouraging me to pursue my own dream. We were sitting in the living room when I showed a new scene that I'd written for a comic solo theatre piece about my time failing in Hollywood. Reuben loved it, he thought it was a breakthrough and even offered to make time to develop it with me. At the time, I thought it was impractical and I had to keep pursuing more commercial, realistic projects. In that moment, in Aileen's living room, Reuben was fighting for my creativity, trying to vanquish all the doubts and mental obstacles holding me back. As the younger, the traditional underdog, he was fighting for that part of me that has never gets attention, that younger, freer, mischievous, defiant spirit that rarely gets a look in.

Ten years on, I realise that Reuben doesn't need me to rescue anyone. The best tribute I can give him is to champion that playful, wild, fighting spirit which was the best of him.

References

Abraham, K. (1988 [1912]) *Selected Papers on Psychoanalysis*. London: Routledge.

Adcock, R.A., & Clarke, E.A. (2011) Spirituality in grief: A model of endogenous and exogenous factors. Omega: *Journal of Death and Dying*, 63(3):235–253.

After the Hijack (1978) David Cohen director, Kit Davies, editor, ATV.

Allen, J.R., Whittlesey, S., Pfefferbaum, B. and Ondersma, M.L. (1999) Community and coping of mothers and grandmothers of children killed in a human-caused disaster. *Psychiatric Annals* 29(2):85–91.

Angelhoff, C., Sveen, J., Alvariza, A., Weber-Falk, M. and Kreicbergs, U. (2021) Communication, self-esteem and prolonged grief in parent-adolescent dyads, 1–4 years following the death of a parent to cancer. *European Journal of Oncology Nursing,* Feb. doi: 10.1016/j.ejon.2020.101883

Augustine of Hippo (2008) *Confessions*. Oxford: Oxford University Press.

Bates, A. and Kearney, J.A. (2015) Understanding death with limited experience in life: dying children's and adolescents' understanding of their own terminal illness and death. *Curr Opin Support Palliat Care.* Mar;9(1):40–45. doi: 10.1097/SPC.0000000000000118

Beckett, S. (2006) *Waiting for Godot*. London: Faber and Faber.

Becvar, D.S. (2000) Families experiencing death, dying, and bereavement. In: Nichols, W.C., Pace-Nichols, M.A. (eds) *Handbook of Family Development and Intervention*. Indianapolis, IN: Wiley, pp. 453–470.

Becvar, D.S. (2003) *In the Presence of Grief*. New York: Guilford Press.

Beeton, I. (2018) *The Book of Household Management*. London: Franklin Classics.

Bell, C.J., Skiles, J., Pradhan, K. and Champion, V.L. (2010) End-of-life experiences in adolescents dying with cancer. *Support Care Cancer,* 18:827–835.

Belsky, J., Caspi, A., Moffitt, T.E. and Poulton, R. (2020) *The Origins of You: How Childhood Shapes Later Life*. Cambridge, MA: Harvard University Press.

Benfield, D.G., Leib, S.A. and Vollman, J.H. (1978) Grief response of parents to neonatal death and parent participation in deciding care. *Pediatrics*, 62(2):171–177.

Biden, J. (2021) *American Dreamer*. London: Bloomsbury.

Blackburn, S. (2001) *Think: A Compelling Introduction to Philosophy*. Oxford: Oxford University Press.

Bluebond-Langner, M. (1978) *The Private Worlds of Dying Children*. Princeton, NJ: Princeton University Press.

Boelen, P.A., Van Den Bout, J., De Keijser, J., and Hoijtink, H. (2003) Reliability and validity of the Dutch version of the inventory of traumatic grief (ITG). *Death Studies,* Apr;27(3):227–247. doi: 10.1080/07481180302889

Bohannon, J. (1991) Grief responses of spouses following the death of a child: a longitudinal study. *Omega: Journal of Death and Dying*, 22:109–121.

Bonanno, G. (2001) Grief and emotion: a social–functional perspective. In: Stroebe, M., Stroebe, W.S. and Hansson, R. (ed.) *Handbook of Bereavement Research*. Washington, DC: American Psychological Association, pp. 493–515.

Bonanno, G. and Field, N. (2001) Examining the delayed grief hypothesis across 5 years of bereavement. *The American Behavioural Scientist*, 44(5):798–816.

Bonanno, G. and Kaltman, S. (1999) Toward an integrative perspective on bereavement. *Psychological Bulletin*, 125:760–776.

Bonanno, G., Worman, C., Lehman, D., Tweed, R., Haring, M., Sonnega, J., Carr, D. and Nesse, R. (2002) Resilience to loss and chronic grief: a prospective study from preloss to 18-months post loss. *Journal of Personality and Social Psychology*, 1150–1164. doi: 10.1037//0022–3514.83.5.1150

Bowlby, J. (1980) *Loss, Sadness, and Depression*. New York: Basic Books.

Brattico, E., Alluri, V., Bogert, B., Jacobsen, T., Vartiainen, N., Nieminen, S., Tervaniemi, M. (2011) A functional MRI study of happy and sad emotions in music with and without lyrics. *Front Psychol.* Dec 1;2:308. doi: 10.3389/fpsyg.2011.00308. PMID: 22144968; PMCID: PMC3227856.

Buckley, T., Sunari, D., Marshall, A., Bartrop, R., McKinley, S. and Tofler, G. (2012) Physiological correlates of bereavement and the impact of bereavement interventions. *Dialogues Clin Neurosci.* Jun;14(2):129–139.

Burke, L.A. and Neimeyer, R.A. (2013) Prospective risk factors in complicated grief. In: Stroebe, *Complicated Grief*. London: Routledge.

Caffey, J. (1965) Significance of the history of the battered child syndrome, *Journal of Paediatrics*, 67:1011ff.

Caffey, J. (2011) Fractures in the long bones of battered infants, *Clinical Orthopaedics*, 469:757ff.

Carson, M. (2010) *Sucking Sherbet Lemons*, London: Cutting Edge.

Centers for Disease Control and Prevention (1997) Rates of homicide, suicide, and firearm related deaths among children: 26 industrialized countries. *Mortality and Morbidity Weekly Report*, 46(7):101–105.

Chang, C. and Fraga, J. (2022) How grief affects your gut health. *Time Magazine*. July 1. https://time.com/6193214/grief-gut-health/

Chen, H., Wei, D., Janszky, I., Dahlström, U., Rostila, M., & László, K. (2022) Bereavement and prognosis in heart failure: a Swedish cohort study. *JACC: Heart Failure*, July 6, 2022.

Christ, G.H., Siegel, K., Mesagno, F.P. and Langosch, D. (1991) A preventive intervention program for bereaved children: problems of implementation. *American Journal of Orthopsychiatry*, 61:168–178.

Christie, A. (2018) *Dumb Witness*. New York: William Morrow.

Cohen, A. (2012) *Le livre de ma mère*. Paris: Gallimard.

Cohen, D. (2013) *Home Alone*. London: Robson Books.

Cohen, D. (2006) *Freud on Coke*. London: Cutting Edge.

Cohen, R. (1999) Relativity and the single male. *Absinthe Literary Review*.

Cohen, R. *Theo's Ruins*, unpublished MS.

Cohen, Reuben with Brenton, S. (2003) *Shooting Reality*. London: Verso.

Conan Doyle, A. (1926) *The History of Spiritualism*. London: Cassell.

Cook, J. (1988) Dad's double binds: rethinking fathers' bereavement from a men's studies perspective. *Journal of Contemporary Ethnography*, 17(3):285–308.

Cooley, C., Adeodu, S., Aldred, H. and Beesley, S. (2000) Paediatric palliative care: A lack of research-based evidence *International Journal of Palliative Nursing*. August. 6(7):346–351 doi:10.12968/ijpn.2000.6.7.9070

Darwin, C. (1859) *On the Origin of Species*. London: John Murray.

Davies, B. (1991) Long term outcomes of adolescent sibling bereavement. *Journal of Adolescent Research*, 6:83–96.

Davies, B. (1993) Sibling bereavement: research-based guidelines for nurses. *Seminars in Oncology Nursing*, 9:107–113.

Davies, B. (1999) *Shadows in the Sun: The Experiences of Sibling Bereavement in Childhood*. Philadelphia, PA: Taylor & Francis.

Davies, D.E. (2006) Parental suicide after the expected death of a child at home *BMJ*. 16th March. 332 doi: 10.1136/bmj.332.7542.64

Dawson, D.A., Li, T.-K.i and Grant, B.F. (2008) A prospective study of risk drinking: at risk for what? *Drug and Alcohol Dependence*, 95(1–2):62–72.

Dawson, D.A. (1998) Lost children, living memories. *Death Studies,* 22:121–140.

DeFrain, J. (1991) Learning about grief from normal families: SIDS, stillbirths, and miscarriages. *Journal of Marital and Family Therapy*, 17:215–223.

DeFrain, J., Martens L., Stork, J., Stork, W. (1991) The psychological effects of a stillbirth on surviving family members. *Omega*, 22:81–108.

de Groot, M., de Keijser, J., Neeleman, J., Kerkhof, A., Nolen, W. and Burger, H. (2007) Cognitive behaviour therapy to prevent complicated grief among relatives and spouses bereaved by suicide: cluster randomised controlled trial. *British Medical Journal*, 334(7601):994.

de Montigny, F., Dumas, L., Beaudet L. (1999) A baby has died: the impact of perinatal loss on family social networks. *Journal of Obstetric, Gynecologic, & Neonatal Nursing*, 28(2):151–156.

D'Espérance, E. (2012) *Shadow Land; or Light from the Other Side*, London: CreateSpace Independent Publishing Platform.

De Vries, M., Lana, R.D. and Falck, V. (1994) Parental bereavement over the life course: a theoretical intersection and empirical review. *Omega,* 29:47–69.

DiMarco, M.A., Menke, E.M., McNamara, T. (2001) Evaluating a support group for parental loss. *American Journal of Maternal and Child Nursing,* 26(3):135–140.

Doering, B.K. and Eisma, M.C. (2016) Treatment for complicated grief: state of the science and ways forward. *Current Opinion in Psychiatry*, 29(5):286–291.

Dunn, S. (2020, Feb. 05) How to smoke and drink your way through grief. *Human Parts*. https://humanparts.medium.com/the-silence-of-a-smoke-filled-bar-68674de7c981

Eisma, M.C., Stroebe, M.S., Schut, H.A., Stroebe, W., Boelen, P.A. and van den Bout. J. (2013). Avoidance processes mediate the relationship between rumination and symptoms of complicated grief and depression following loss. *Journal of Abnormal Psychology*, 122(4): 961–970.

Emmons, R.A., Colby, P.M. and Kaiser, H.A. (1998) When losses lead to gains: personal goals and the recovery of meaning. In: Wong, P.T.P. and Fry, P.S. (eds) *The Human Quest for Meaning: A Handbook of Psychological Research and Clinical Applications*. Mahwah, NJ: Erlbaum, pp. 163–178.

Evelyn, J. (2006) *The Diaries of John Evelyn*. London: Everyman.

Fagundes, C. (2020) Matters of the heart: grief and morbidity. *Current Directions in Psychological Science,* 49(3):235–241.

Fanos, J. and Nickerson, B. (1991) Long-term effects of sibling death during adolescence. *Journal of Adolescent Research*, 6:70–82.

Ferris, E. (2020, May 14) *Understanding the pain of grief.* The Breath Effect Blog.

Field, M. and Berhman, R. (eds) (2003) *When Children Die: Improving Palliative and End-of-Life Care for Children and Their Families.* Washington, DC: National Academies Press.

Finkbeiner, A. (2021) The biology of grief, *The New York Times* Apr. 22. https://www.nytimes.com/2021/04/22/well/what-happens-in-the-body-during-grief.html

Fish, W. 1986, Differences of grief intensity in bereaved parents, In: Rando, T. (ed.) *Parental Loss of a Child.* Champaign, IL: Research Press, pp. 415–428.

Fitzgerald, H. (1992) *The Grieving Child: A Parent's Guide.* Washington, DC: Simon & Schuster.

Frankl, V.E. (1978) *The Unheard Cry for Meaning: Psychotherapy and Humanism.* New York: Simon & Schuster.

Freeman, L., Shafer, D. and Smith, H. (1996) Neglected victims of homicide: the needs of young siblings of murder victims. *American Journal of Orthopsychiatry,* 66(3):337–345.

Freeman, L. (1998) Clinical issues in assessment and intervention with children and adolescents exposed to homicide. In: Rando, T. (ed.) *Promoting Cultural Competence in Children's Mental Health Services: Systems of Care for Children's Mental Health.* Baltimore, MD: Brookes Publishing.

Freud, S. (1957[1915]) *Mourning and Melancholia.* London: Hogarth Press.

Freud, S. (1922) *The Pleasure Principle.* London: Hogarth Press.

Freud, S. with Einstein, A. (1933) *Why War?* League of Nations pamphlet.

Friedman, S.H. and Resnick, P.J. (2007) Child murder by mothers: patterns and prevention. *World Psychiatry,* 6(3):137–141.

Gibbons, M. (1992) A child dies, a child survives: the impact of sibling loss. *Journal of Pediatric Health Care,* 6: 72–76.

Gilbert, K. (1997) Couple coping with the death of a child. In: Figley, C., Bride, B. and Mazza, N. (eds) *Death and Trauma.* Washington, DC and London: Taylor & Francis, pp. 101–121.

Goethe (2015) *Collected Works.* Princeton, NJ: Princeton University Press.

Grollman, E. (1995) *Bereaved Children and Teens.* Boston, MA: Beacon Press.

Grossman, D. (2006) Eulogy for his son. *The Guardian,* 18 August.

Hackett, J., and Beresford, B. (2021) 'Cold bedrooms' and other cooling facilities in UK children's hospices, how they are used and why they are offered: A mixed methods study. *Palliat Med.* Mar;35(3):603–610. doi: 10.1177/0269216320984335

Haupt, L. (2006) *Pilgrim on the Great Bird Continent: The Importance of Everything and Other Lessons from Darwin's Lost Notebooks.* New York: Little Brown.

Hauser, R.M., Carr, D., Hauser, T.S., Krecher, M., Kuo, D., Presti, J., Shinberg, D. et al. (1993) *The Class of 1957 after 35 Years: Overview and Preliminary Findings.* Madison, WI: University of Wisconsin – Madison, Center for Demography and Ecology (Working Paper No. 93-17).

Hazzard, A., Weston, J. and Gutterres, C. (1992). After a child's death: Factors related to parental bereavement. *Journal of Developmental and Behavioral Pediatrics,* 13(1), 24–30. doi: 10.1097/00004703-199202000-00006

Hicklenton, J. (2010) *100 Months.* London: Cutting Edge.

Hogan, N. and Balk, D. (1990) Adolescent reactions to sibling death: perceptions of mothers, fathers, and teenagers. *Nursing Research,* 39(2):103–106.

Hogan, N. and DeSantis, L. (1994) Things that help and hinder adolescent sibling bereavement. *Western Journal of Nursing Research,* 16(2):132–153.

Hopf, D., Eckstein, M., Aguilar-Raab, C., Warth, M. and Ditzen, B. (2020) Neuroendocrine mechanisms of grief and bereavement: a systematic review and implications for future interventions. *Journal of Neuroendocrinology,* 32(8):e12887.

Houghton, G. (2013) *Evenings at Home in Spiritual Séance.* London: Victorian Secrets.

Hu, H., Shear, B.A., Thakkar, R., Thompson Lastad, A., Pinderhughes, H., Hecht, F. and Lown, F.A (2019) Acupressure and therapeutic touch in childhood cancer to promote subjective and intersubjective experiences of well-being during curative treatment. *Global Advances in Health and Medicine,* 8(1). doi:10.1177/2164956119880143

Hughes, C. and Page-Lieberman, J. (1989) Fathers experiencing a perinatal loss. *Death Studies,* 13:537–556.

Hurcombe, L. (2004) *Losing a Child,* London: Sheldon Press.

Hurcombe, L. (2007) *Depression: Healing Emotional Distress.* London: Sheldon Press.

Hutton, C. and Bradley, B. (1994) Effects of sudden infant death on bereaved siblings: A comparative study. *Journal of Child Psychology and Psychiatry,* 35:723–732.

Infurna, F. and Luthar, S. (2017) Parents' adjustment following the death of their child: resilience is multidimensional and differs across outcomes examined. *Journal of Research in Personality,* 68: 38–53.

James, W. (1902) *Varieties of Religious Experience.* Chicago: Riverside Press.

Jay, S.M., Green, V., Johnson, S. et al. (1987) Differences in death concepts between children with cancer and physically healthy children. *Journal of Clinical Child & Adolescent Psychology,* 16:301–306.

Jenkin, L. (1703) *Memoir of William Duke of Gloucester.* London: Payne.

Jones, E. (1957) *Life and Work of Sigmund Freud.* New York: Basic Books.

Jones, M.P., Bartrop, R.W. and Forcier, L. (2010) Concordance between sources of morbidity reports. *Self-Reports and Medical Records,* 2:16 doi: 10.3389/fphar.2011.00016

Johnson, S. (1987) *After a Child Dies: Counselling Bereaved Families.* New York: Springer.

Jonson, B. (2021) *The Poems of Ben Jonson.* London: Routledge.

Joyce, J. (2006) *Ulysses.* Penguin Classics. London: Penguin.

Kazak, A.E. and Noll, R.B. (2004) Child death from paediatric illness: conceptualizing intervention from a family/systems and public health perspective. *Professional Psychology: Research and Practice,* 35:219–226.

Kazak, A.E., Lamia P.B., Alderfer, M., Rourke, M., Meeske, K., Gallagher, A.C., Cnaan, A. and Stuber, M.L. (2001) Post-traumatic stress in survivors of childhood cancer and mothers: development and validation of the impact of traumatic stressors interview schedule (ITSIS). *Journal of Clinical Psychology in Medical Settings,* 8(4):307–323.

Keats, J. (1977) Complete Poems. Penguin Classics. Harmondsworth: Penguin.

Kempe, C.H., Silverman, F.N., Steele, B.F., Droegemueller, W. and Silver, H.K. (1984) The Battered Baby Syndrome. *Journal of the American Medical Association,* 251(24):3288–3294. doi: 10.1001/jama.251.24.3288

Kersting, A., Brähler, E., Glaesmer, and Wagner, B. (2011) Prevalence of complicated grief in a representative population-based sample. *Journal of Affective Disorders,* 131(1–3):339–343.

Kicking the Habit (1985) ITV film.

Kipling, R. (1894) *The Jungle Book.* London: Macmillan.

Kipling, R. (1994) *Collected Poems.* London: Macmillan.

Klass, D. (1997) Marriage and divorce among bereaved parents in a self-help group. *Omega: Journal of Death and Dying,* 17:237–249.

Klass, D. (1999) *The Spiritual Lives of Bereaved Parents.* Philadelphia, PA: Brunner/Mazel.

Krisch (2019) Data shows the death of a child changes parents forever. *Fatherly*. https://www.yahoo.com/lifestyle/data-shows-death-child-changes-222036895.html

Kubler-Ross, E. (2003*) On Death and Dying*. New York: Simon & Schuster.

Kubler-Ross, E. (1975) *Death and the Final Stage of Growth*. Englewood Cliffs, NJ: Prentice Hall, Inc.

Lang, A. and Gottlieb L. (1991) Marital intimacy in bereaved and nonbereaved couples: a comparative study, In: Papadatou, D. and Papadatos, C. (eds) *Children and Death*. New York: Hemisphere Publishing Corporation, pp. 267–275.

Lang, A. and Gottlieb, L. (1993) Parental grief reactions and marital intimacy following infant deaths. *Death Studies*, 20:33–57.

Lannen, P.K., Wolfe, J., Prigerson, H., Onelove, E. and Kreigsberg, U. (2008) Unresolved grief in a national sample of bereaved parents: impaired mental and physical health 4 to 9 years later. *Journal of Clinical Oncology*, 26(36): 5870–5876. doi: 10.1200/JCO.2007.14.6738

Larkin, Philip. (1988) "An Arundel Tomb", *Collected Poems*, Faber and Faber.

Leader, D. (2009) *The New Black: Mourning, Melancholia and Depression*. London: Penguin.

Lehman, D.R., Wortman, C.B. and Williams, A.F. (1987) Long-term effects of losing a spouse or child in a motor vehicle crash. *Journal of Personality and Social Psychology*, 52:218–231.

Lepore, S., Camille, B., Wortman, C.B., Cohen Silver, R. and Wayment, H. (1996) Social constraints, intrusive thoughts, and depressive symptoms among bereaved mothers. *Journal of Personality and Social Psychology*, 70(2):271–282.

Lertzman, R. (2010) On loss and mourning. *The Psychologist*, July 20. The British Psychological Society.

Lettieri, R. (2021) Why do parents kill children? *Psychology Today*, April 27.

Li, J., Precht, D.H., Mortenson, P.B. and Olson, J. (2003). Mortality in parents after death of a child in Denmark: a nation-wide follow-up study. *Lancet*, 361:363–367.

Li, J., Laursen, T.M., Precht, D.H., Olsen, J. and Mortensen, P.B. (2005) Hospitalization for mental illness among parents after the death of a child. *New England Journal of Medicine*, 352:1190–1196.

Lindemann, E. (1944) Symptomatology and management of acute grief. *American Journal of Psychiatry*, 101:141–149.

Listermar, K.H., Sormunen, T. and Rådestad, I. (2020) Perinatal palliative care after a stillbirth – Midwives' experiences of using Cubitus baby, *Women and Birth*, Volume 33: 2, 161–164. doi.org/10.1016/j.wombi.2019.05.013

Lowman, J. (1979) Grief intervention and sudden infant death syndrome. *American Journal of Community Psychology*, 7:665–667.

Maccallum, F., Isaac, R., Galatzer-Levy, I ., George, A. and Bonanno, G. (2015) Trajectories of depression following spousal and child bereavement: a comparison of the heterogeneity in outcomes. *Journal of Medical Ethics*, 33(4):194–196. doi: 10.1136/jme.2006.016360

Malacrida, C.A. (1992) Perinatal death: helping parents find their way, *Journal of Family Nursing* 3(2): 130–149. doi: 10.1177/107484079700300203

Malkinson, R. and Bar-Tuv, L. (1999) The aging of grief in Israel: a perspective of bereaved parents. *Death Studies*, 23(6):413–431.

Malkinson, R., Rubin, S. and Witztum, E. (eds) (2000) *Traumatic and Nontraumatic Loss and Bereavement: Clinical Theory and Practice*. Madison, CT: Psychosocial Press.

Mandell, F., McAnulty, E. and Reece, R. (1980) Observations of parental response to sudden unanticipated infant death. *Pediatrics*, 65:221–225.

Manseau, P. (2017) *The Apparitionists: A Tale of Phantoms, Fraud, Photography, and the Man Who Captured Lincoln's Ghost*. Boston, MA: Houghton Mifflin Harcourt.

Mariano, T.Y., Chan, H.C.(O). and Myers, W.C. (2014) Toward a more holistic under-standing of filicide: A multidisciplinary analysis of 32 years of US arrest data. *Forensic Science International,* 236:46–53.

Martinson, I. and Campos, R. (1991) Adolescent bereavement: long term responses to a sibling's death from cancer. *Journal of Adolescent Research,* 7:54–69.

Martinson, I., Davies, B. and McClowry, S. (1991) Parental depression following the death of a child. *Death Studies,* 15:359–367.

McClowry, S.G., Davies, E.B., May, K.A., Kulenkamp, E.J. and Martinson, I.M. (1995) The empty space phenomenon: the process of grief in the bereaved family. In: Doka, K.J. (ed.) *Children Mourning, Mourning Children.* Washington, DC: Hospice Foundation of America, pp. 149–162.

McCreight, B. (2004) A grief ignored: narratives of pregnancy loss from a male perspective, *Sociology of Health and Illness.* Apr;26(3):326–350. doi: 10.1111/j.1467-9566.2004.00393.x

McCullough, M. (2008) *Beyond Revenge: The Evolution of the Forgiveness Instinct.* San Francisco: Jossey Bass.

Mills-Koonce, W.R., Garrett-Peters, P., Barnett, M., Granger, D.A., Blair, C., Cox, M.J. and Family Life Key Investigators (2011) Father contributions to cortisol responses in infancy and toddlerhood. *Dev Psychol.* Mar;47(2):388–395. doi: 10.1037/a0021066

Mitterschiffthaler, M.T., Fu, C.H.Y., Dalton, J.A., Andrew, C.M. and Williams, S.C.R. (2007) A functional MRI study of happy and sad affective states induced by classical music, *Human Brain Mapping,* 28, 1150–1162. doi: 10.1002/hbm.20337

Munro, E. (2011) *The Munro Review of Child Protection.* Department of Education. London.

Murphy, S.A., Johnson, L.C., Wu, L., Fan, J.J. and Lohan, J. (2003) Bereaved parents' outcomes 4 to 60 months after their children's deaths by accident, suicide, or homicide: a comparative study demonstrating differences. *Death Studies,* 27:39–61.

Murray, J. and Callan, V. (1988) Predicting adjustment to perinatal death. *British Journal of Medical Psychology,* 61:237–244.

Nader, K. (1996) Children's exposure to traumatic experiences. In: Corr, C. and Corr, D. (eds) *Handbook of Childhood Death and Bereavement.* pp. 201–220. Springer Publishing Co. New York.

Nader, K. (1997) Childhood traumatic loss: interaction of trauma and grief, In: Figley, C., Bride, B. and Mazza, N. (eds) *Death and Trauma: The Traumatology of Grieving.* New York: Hamilton Printing Company, pp.17–41.

Nagy, M. (1948) The child's theories concerning death. *Journal of Genetic Psychology,* 73:3–27.

Najman, J.M., Vance, J.C., Boyle, F, Embleton, G., Foster, B. and Thearle, J. (1993) The impact of child death on marital adjustment. *Social Sciences Medicine,* 37:1005–1010.

Neimeyer, R.A. (1998) *Lessons of Loss: A Guide to Coping.* New York: McGraw-Hill.

Neimeyer, R.A. (2001a) *Meaning, Reconstruction and the Experience of Loss.* Washington, DC: American Psychological Association.

Neimeyer, R.A. (2001b) Reauthoring life narratives: grief therapy as meaning reconstruc-tion. *Israel Journal of Psychiatry and Related Sciences,* 38(3–4):171–183.

Neimeyer, R.A., Keese, N. and Fortner, B. (2000) Loss and meaning reconstruction: propo-sitions and procedures. In Malkinson, R., Rubin, S.S. and Witztum, E. (eds), *Traumatic and Nontraumatic Loss and Bereavement: Clinical Theory and Practice.* Madison, CT: Psycho-social Press, pp. 197–230.

Nelson, B.J. and Frantz. T.T. (1996) Family interactions of suicide survivors and survivors of non-suicidal death. *Omega,* 33:131–146.

NSPCC Digest (2022) *A Review of Child Deaths.* London: NSPCC.

O'Brien, S. (1979) *The Negative Scream.* London: Routledge.

O'Connor, F. (2022) *The Grieving Brain*. London: Harper One.

Oliver, L.E. (1999) Effects of a child's death on the marital relationship: a review. *Omega: Journal of Death and Dying,* 39:197–227.

Ouija (2014) film directed by Stiles White.

Parkes, C.M. (1998) *Bereavement: Studies of Grief in Adult Life,* 3rd edn. Madison, CT: International Universities Press.

Parkes, C.M. and Weiss, R. (1983) *Recovery from Bereavement*. Basic Books. New York.

Pathways (2023) How to manage emotional eating during the grieving process. https://pathwayshealth.org/grief-support/how-to-manage-emotional-eating-during-the-grieving-process/

Peach, M. and Klass, D. (1987) Special issues in the grief of parents of murdered children. *Death Studies,* 11:81–88, 99.

Piaget, J. (2001) *The Language and Thought of the Child*. London: Routledge.

Pilling, J., Konkolÿ-Thege, B., Demetrovics, Z. and Kopp, M.S. (2012) Alcohol use in the first three years of bereavement: a national representative survey. *Substance Abuse Treatment, Prevention,* Jan. 16;7:3. doi: 10.1186/1747-597X-7-3

Pius XII (1950) *Munificentissimus Deus encyclical.*

Plutarch (1919) *Cicero*. Cambridge, MA: Loeb Classical Library.

Powell, M. (1991) The psychological impact of sudden infant death syndrome on siblings. *Irish Journal of Psychology,* 12:235–247.

Prigerson, H.G., Bierhals, A.J., Kasl, S.V., Reynolds, C.F. III, Shear, M.K., Newsom, J.T. and Jacobs, S. (1996) Complicated grief as a disorder distinct from bereavement-related depression and anxiety: a replication study. *American Journal of Psychiatry,* 153:1484–1486.

Prigerson, H.G., Bierhals, A.J., Kasl, S.V, Reynolds, C.F. III, Shear, M.K., Newsom, J.T. and Jacobs, S. (1996). Complicated grief as a disorder distinct from bereavement-related depression and anxiety: a replication study. *American Journal of Psychiatry,* 153, 1484–1486.

Prigerson, H.G., Shear, M.K., Jacobs, S.C., Reynolds, C.F., Maciejewski, P.K., Davidson, J.R.T. and Rosenheck, R. (1999) Consensus criteria for traumatic grief: a preliminary empirical test. *British Journal of Psychiatry,* 174:67–73.

Prigerson, H.G. and Jacobs, S.C. (2001a) Caring for bereaved patients: all the doctors just suddenly go. *Journal of the American Medical Association,* 286(11):1369–1376.

Prigerson, H.G. and Jacobs S.C. (2001b) Traumatic grief as a distinct disorder: A rationale, consensus criteria, and a preliminary empirical test. In: M. S. Stroebe, R. O. Hansson, W. Stroebe, & H. Schut (eds) *Handbook of Bereavement Research: Consequences, Coping, and Care*. American Psychological Association, pp. 613–645. doi: 10.1037/10436-026

Pynoos, R. and Nader, K. (1988) Psychological first aid and treatment approach to children exposed to community violence: research implications. *Journal of Traumatic Stress,* 1(4):445–473.

Radfar, A., Abohashem, A., Osborne, M., Wang, Y., Dar, T., Hassan, M., Ghoneem, A., Naddaf, N., Patrich, T. and Abbasi, T. (2021) Stress-associated neurobiological activity associates with the risk for and timing of subsequent Takotsubo syndrome *European Heart Journal,* May 14;42(19): 1898–1908. doi: 10.1093/eurheartj/ehab029

Radloff, L.S. (1997) The CES-D Scale: a self-report depression scale for research in the general population. *Applied Psychological Measurement* 1:385–401.

Ramsden, R. (2012) *Murder at the Blue Parrot*, London: Cutting Edge.

Rando, T. (1991) Parental adjustment to the loss of a child. In: Papadatou, D. and Papadatos, C. (eds) *Children and Death*. New York: Hemisphere Publishing Company, pp. 233–252.

Rando, T. (1993) *Treatment of Complicated Mourning*. Champaign, IL: Research Press.

Rando, T. (1996) Complications of mourning traumatic death. In: Dolca, K. (ed.) *Living with Grief and Sudden Loss*. Washington, DC: Hospice Foundation of America, pp. 139–160.

Reilly-Smorawski, B., Armstrong, A. and Catlin, E. (2002) Bereavement support for couples following death of a baby: program development and 14-year exit analysis. *Death Studies*, 26(1):21–37. doi: 10.1080/07481180210145

Robinson, C. and Jackson, P. (1999) Children's hospices: where do they fit? *Critical Social Policy*, 23(1). doi: 10.1177/026101830302300106

Rogers, C., Floyd, F., Seltzer, M., Greenberg, J. and Hong, J. (2008) Long-term effects of the death of a child on parents' adjustment in midlife, *Journal of Family Psychiatry*, 22: 203–211. doi: 10.1037/0893–3200.22.2.203

Rosen, H. (1985) Prohibitions against mourning in childhood sibling loss. *Omega*, 15:307–316.

Rosenberg, A.R., Orellana, L., Kang, T.I. et al. (2014) Differences in parent-provider concordance regarding prognosis and goals of care among children with advanced cancer. *Journal of Clinical Oncology*, 32:3005–3011.

Rosenblatt, P.C. (2001) A social constructionist perspective on cultural differences in grief. In: Stroebe, M.S., Hansson, R.O., Stroebe, W. and Schut, H. (eds) *Handbook of Bereavement Research: Consequences, Coping, and Care*. Washington, DC: American Psychological Association. doi: 10.1037/10436-012

Rubin, S. (1981) The two-track model of bereavement: theory and research. *American Journal of Orthopsychiatry*, 51(1):101–109.

Rubin, S. (1993) The death of a child is forever: the life course impact of child loss. In: Stroebe, M.S., Stroebe, R.O. and Hansson, W. (eds) *Handbook of Bereavement: Theory, Research, and Intervention*. Cambridge: Cambridge University Press, pp. 285–299.

Rubin, S. (1999) The two-track model of bereavement: overview, retrospect and prospect. *Death Studies*, 23(8):681–714.

Rubin, S. and Malkinson, R. (2001) Parental response to child loss across the life cycle: clinical and research perspectives, In: Stroebe, M. (ed). *Handbook of Bereavement Research: Consequences, Coping, and Care*. Washington, DC: American Psychological Association Press, pp. 219–240.

Rubin, S. and Schechter, N. (1997) Exploring the social construction of bereavement: perceptions of adjustment and recovery for bereaved men. *American Journal of Orthopsychiatry*, 67(2):279–289.

Rutter, M. (1994) Stress research: accomplishments and tasks ahead, In: Hagerty, R. (ed.) *Stress, Risk and Resilience in Children and Adolescents*. Cambridge: Cambridge University Press, pp. 354–385.

Samuelsson, M., Rådestad, I. and Segesten, K. (2001) A waste of life: fathers' experience of losing a child before birth. *Birth: Issues in Perinatal Care*, 28(2), 124–130. doi: 10.1046/j.1523-536X.2001.00124.x

Sanders, C. (1979–1980) A comparison of adult bereavement in the death of a spouse, child, and parent. *Omega*, 10: 303–322.

Sanders, C. (1989) *Grief: The Mourning After*. New York: John Wiley & Sons.

Schiff, H. (1977) *The Bereaved Parent*. New York: Penguin Books.

Schmutte, P.S. and Ryff, C.D. (1997) Personality and well-being: reexamining methods and meanings. *Journal of Personality and Social Psychology*, 73:549–559.

Schrag, M. (2003) *Walking through the Valley of the Shadow: When a Jewish Child Dies*. Ritualwell. https://ritualwell.org/ritual/excerpts-walking-through-valley-shadow-when-jewish-child-dies/.

Schreiner, R., Greshman, E. and Green, M. (1979) Physician's responsibility to parents after death of an infant: beneficial outcomes of a telephone call. *American Journal of Diseases of Children*, 133:723–726.

Schut, H., Stroebe, M.S., van den Bout, J. and Terheggen, M. (2001). The efficacy of bereavement interventions: Determining who benefits. In: M. S. Stroebe, R.O. Hansson, W. Stroebe and H. Schut (eds), *Handbook of Bereavement Research: Consequences, Coping, and Care* (pp. 705–737). American Psychological Association. doi:10.1037/10436-029

Schwab, R. (1992) Effects of a child's death on the marital relationship: a preliminary study. *Death Studies*, 16:141–154.

Scottish Government (2014) Key Information on the Use of Antidepressants in Scotland. Published 29 July.

Seltzer, M.M., Greenberg, J.S., Floyd, F.J., Pettee, Y. and Hong, J. (2001) Life course impacts of parenting a child with a disability. *American Journal on Mental Retardation*, 106:265–286.

Shear, S.B. (2015) Manifesting destiny: re/presentations of indigenous peoples in K–12 U.S. history standards. *Theory and Research in Social Education*, 43(1):68–101 doi: 10.1080/00933104.2014.999849

Shear, M.K., Reynolds, C.F. 3rd, Simon, N.M., Zisook. S., Wang. Y, Mauro, C., Duan, N., Lebowitz, B., Skritskaya, N. (2016) Optimizing treatment of complicated grief: a randomized clinical trial. *JAMA Psychiatry*. Jul 1;73(7):685–694. doi: 10.1001/jamapsychiatry.2016.0892

Sherkat, D.E. and Reed, M.D. (1992) The effects of religion and social support on self-esteem and depression among the suddenly bereaved. *Social Indicators Research*, 26:259–275.

Siegel, K., Mesagno, R. and Christ, G. (1990) A preventive program for bereaved children. *American Journal of Orthopsychiatry*, 60:168–175.

Silverman, F. (1953) The Roentgen Manifestation of unrecognised skeletal trauma in infants. *American Journal of Roentology*, 69:4313–4322.

Song, J., Floyd, F.J., Seltzer, M.M., Greenberg, J.S. and Hong, J. (2010) Long-term effects of child death on parents' health related quality of life: a dyadic analysis. *Fam Relat*. Jul 1; 59(3): 269–282. doi: 10.1111/j.1741-3729.2010.00601.x

Sourkes, B.M. (1995) *Armfuls of Time: The Psychological Experience of the Child with a Life-Threatening Illness*. Pittsburgh, PA: University of Pittsburgh Press, pp. xiv, 187–216.

Souvik, R. 13 signs that show the spirit world is trying to make contact with you. *India Times*. Feb. 03. https://www.indiatimes.com/lifestyle/self/13-signs-that-show-the-spirit-world-is-trying-to-make-contact-with-you-238617.html

Spielberger, C.D. (1983) *Manual for STAI*. Palo Alto, CA: Mind Garden.

Spour, H. (2017) The hard truth about staying married after losing a child. *Huffington Post*. https://www.huffpost.com/entry/the-hard-truth-about-staying-married-after-losing-a-child_b_5606847

Stehbens, J.A. and Lascari, A.D. (1974) Psychological follow-up of families with childhood leukemia. *Journal of Clinical Psychology*, 30:394–397.

Steinbaum, S. (2016) interviewed by Nancy Lonsdorf, February 16th. https://drlonsdorf.com/2016/02/16/heart-health-interview-with-dr-suzanne-steinbaum/

Stephen, A. I., Macduff, C., Petrie, D. J., Tseng, F. M., Schut, H., Skår, S., Wilson, S. (2015). The economic cost of bereavement in Scotland. *Death Studies*, 39(3), 151–157. doi: 10.1080/07481187.2014.920435

Stroebe (1998) Chapter 16. https://journals.sagepub.com/doi/10.1191/026921698668142811

Stroebe, M. and Schut, H. (2001) Models of coping with bereavement: a review. In Stroebe, M.S., Hansson, R.O., Stroebe, W. and Schut, H. (eds.), *Handbook of Bereavement Research:*

Consequences, Coping, and Care (pp. 375–403). Washington, DC: American Psychological Association. doi: 10.1037/10436-016

Stroebe, M., Schut, H. and Finkenauer, C. (2001) The traumatization of grief? A conceptual framework for understanding the trauma-bereavement interface. *Israeli Journal of Psychiatry and Related Science,* 38(3–4):185–201.

Stroebe, M., Stroebe, W. and Abakoumkin, G. (2005) The broken heart: suicidal ideation in bereavement. *American Journal of Psychiatry,* 162(11):2178–2180. doi: 10.1176/appi. ajp.162.11.2178

Stroebe, M., Stroebe, W. and Hansson, R. (eds) (1993) *Handbook of Bereavement: Theory, Research, and Intervention.* New York: Cambridge University Press.

Stroebe, M., Finkenauer, S.M., Wijngaards-de-Meij, C., Schut, H. Van Den Bout, J., and Stroebe, W. (2013) Partner-oriented self-regulation among bereaved parents: the costs of holding in grief for the partner's sake. *Psychological Science,* 24(4), 395–402. doi: 10.1177/0956797612457383

Strout, E. (2022) *Oh William!* London: Penguin.

Tang-Her, J., Tsay, P.-K., En-Chen, F., Shu-Ho, Y., Shih-Hsiang, C., Chao-Ping, Y. and Iou-Jih, H. (2007) "Do-not-resuscitate" orders in patients with cancer at a children's hospital in Taiwan. *Journal of Medical Ethics.* 33(4):194–196.

Terkel, S. (1988) *The Great Divide.* New York: Avon Books.

Texas House Committee Report on Uvalde (2022) Houston, TX: Texas House of Representatives. https://house.texas.gov/_media/pdf/committees/reports/87interim/Robb-Elementary-Investigative-Committee-Report.pdf

The Compassionate Friends (1999) *When a Child Dies: A Survey of Bereaved Parents.* London: NHS England.

The Favourite (2018) film, directed by Yorgos Lanthimos.

Theunissen, J.M., Hoogerbrugge, P.M., van Achterberg, T. et al. (2007) Symptoms in the palliative phase of children with cancer. *Pediatric Blood Cancer,* 49(2):160–165.

Theunissen, N., Vogels, T., Koopman, H., Verrips, G., Zwinderman, K., Verloove-Vanhorick, S. and Wit, J. (1998) The proxy problem: child report versus parent report in health-related quality of life research. *Quality of Life Research,* 7(5):387–397.

Things Heard and Seen (2021) film directed by Berman and Pulcini.

University of York, (n.d.) The Early Days Project: parents' experiences of the early days of bereavement and the support they receive from children's hospices. https://www.york.ac.uk/spru/projects/early-days-martin-house/

US Secret Service National Threat Assessment Center (2019) Protecting America's schools: A US Secret Service analysis of targeted school violence. https://www.secretservice.gov/sites/default/files/2020-04/Protecting_Americas_Schools.pdf

Van Oudenhove, L., McKie, S., Lassman, D., Uddin, B., Paine, P., Coen, S., Gregory L., Tack, J. and Aziz, Q. (2011) Fatty acid-induced gut-brain signaling attenuates neural and behavioral effects of sad emotion in humans. *J Clin Invest.* Aug;121(8):3094–3099. doi: 10.1172/JCI46380. Epub 2011 Jul 25. PMID: 21785220; PMCID: PMC3148741.

Videka-Sherman, L. (1982) Coping with the death of a child: a study over time. *American Journal of Orthopsychiatry,* 52:688–698.

Voltaire (2006) *Candide.* Harmondsworth: Penguin Classics.

Washington Post (2013) Counseling center cares for people with 'complicated grief', 13 Jan.

Weiss, D.S., and Marmar, C.R. (1997) The Impact of Event Scale-Revised. In: J.P. Wilson and T.M. Keane (eds), *Assessing Psychological Trauma and PTSD*, pp. 399–411. New York: Guilford Press.

Wells, K. (2001) *Goodbye Dearest Holly.* London: Psychology News Press.

Wheeler, I. (2001) Parental bereavement: the crisis of meaning. *Death Studies,* 25:51–61.

Wilde, O. (1895) *The Importance of Being Earnest,* New York: Samuel French.

Williams, T. (2004) (first performed 1955) *Cat on a Hot Tin Roof.* New Directions Publishing.

Winnicott, D.W. (2021) *The Child, the Family and the Outside World.* Penguin Modern Classics. London: Penguin.

Wing, D. Burg-Callaway, K., Clance, P., and Armistead, L. (2001) Understanding gender differences in bereavement following the death of an infant: implications for treatment. *Psychotherapy,* 38(1):60–73.

Wingfield, K., Petit, M. and Klempner, T. (1999) *Mortality Trends among U.S. Children and Youth.* Washington, DC: Child Welfare League of America.

Wijngaards-de Meij, L., Stroebe, M. and Dijkstra, I. (2007) Patterns of attachment and parents' adjustment to the death of their child, *Personality and Social Psychology Bulletin,* Volume 33, issue 4. doi: https://doi.org/10.1177/0146167206297400

Wijngaards-de Meij, L., Stroebe, M., Stroebe, W., Schut, H., Van Den Bout, J., Van Der Hiejden, P.G.M. and Dijkstra, I. (2008) The impact of circumstances surrounding the death of a child on parents' grief. *Death Studies,* 32(3): 237–252. doi: 10.1080/074811807 01881263

Wisconsin Longitudinal Study (2011) Washington, DC: National Institute of Aging.

Witcover, J. (2010) *Joe Biden.* New York: William Morrow.

Wolfe, J., Klar, N. and Grier, H.E. (2000) Understanding of prognosis among parents of children who died of cancer: impact on treatment goals and integration of palliative care. *Journal of the American Medical Association,* 284(19):2469–2475.

Wolfelt, A. (1996) *Healing the Bereaved Child.* Fort Collins, CO: Companion Press.

Woolley, P. and Evans, W. (1955) Significance of skeletal lesions in infants. *Journal of the American Medical Association,* 158, 539–543.

Worden, J. (1996) *Children and Grief: When a Parent Dies.* New York: Guilford Press.

Worth, N. J (1997) Becoming a father to a stillborn child. *Clinical Nursing Research,* 6(1). doi: 10.1177/105477389700600107

Yassenoff, E. (2018, May 23) Bereaved dads are brave dads. *Still Standing Magazine.*

Zadeh, S., Pao, M. and Wiener, L. (2015) Opening end-of-life discussions: how to introduce Voicing My CHOiCES™, an advance care planning guide for adolescents and young adults. *Palliative Support Care,* 13(3):591–599. doi: 10.1017/S1478951514000054

Zeanah, Jr., C.H., and Boris, N.W. (2000) Disturbances and disorders of attachment in early childhood. In: Zeanah, Jr., C.H. (ed.) *Handbook of Infant Mental Health,* New York: Guilford Press, pp. 353–368.

Zelauskas, B. (1981) Siblings: the forgotten grievers. *Issues in Comprehensive Paediatric Nursing,* 5:45–52.

Zisook, S. and Lyons, L. (1989) Bereavement and unresolved grief in psychiatric outpatients. *Omega: Journal of Death and Dying,* 20(4):307–322.

Index

Indexes involve making choices. As this book is about Reuben, myself (David) and grief it seems unnecessary to offer index entries for these as they permeate the whole text.

Jordan, Jan 60
Judaism 3, 93–94

Kaddish 2
Kamrap, Panya 66
Kazak, A.E. 87
Keats, John 8
Kempe, C.H. 67
Kersting, A. 112
Kidron, Beeban 95
Kipling, John 20
Kipling, Josephine 20
Kipling, Rudyard 19–20
Klar, N. 38
Klass, D. 86–87, 91
Klebold, Dylan 60
Kreicbergs, U. 21
Kubler-Ross, Elisabeth 5, 111

Lafferty, Erica 57
Lagone, Elizabeth 96–97
Land, Sonia 12, 34
Lanza, Adam 57
Larkin, Philip 34
László, K. 76
La Tourette, Adele 84
La Tourette, Aileen 3, 7, 14, 28, 31, 84,
    89, 115
La Tourette, Amelie and her husband
    Ralph 14
La Tourette, William 10
Lascari, A.D. 85, 88
Lasky, R. 59
Lawley, Iris 25–26
Lawley, Joe 25–26
Leader, Darien 31–32, 37–38, 43–45, 49,
    113
Lefever, Sarah 32
Lehman, D.R. 86
Leopold Loewenthal, Harold 87
Lettieri, R. 82–83
Li, T. 85, 89
Lincoln, Mary 45
Liverpool Cemetery 1, 6, 84
Liverpool Echo, The 32
Luthar, S. 74
Lyons, L. 112

MacKeith, James 54
Malacrida, C.A. 110
Manseau, P. 45
Manson, Charles 61
Mariano, T. 71
marriage 83, 85, 99–101
Marshall Andrews, G. 55

Martinez, Javier 62–63
Mary, the Virgin 92
Mattei, Chris 57
McClowry, S. 86
McCreight, B. 109
McCullough, M. 107
Mills-Koonce, W.R. 108
Moffitt, T.E. 50
mothers 10, 39, 73, 74, 77, 85, 87, 88, 91,
    99, 100, 107–108, 109, 110, 112
Mourning and Melancholia 21–22
Mumler, W.H. 45
Munro, Eileen 69–71
Murder at the Blue Parrot 12
Murphy, S.A. 86
Murray, Andy 54
Myers, W.C. 71

Nagy, M. 38
Najman, J.M. 88
National Child Traumatic Stress Network 64
National Threat Assessment Centre 53–54,
    64–66
Neimeyer, R.A. 115
New York Times 53
Nietzsche, Friedrich 9
Nogayev, E. 56
Noll, R.B. 87
NSPCC 67–71, 73

O'Brien, Sally 96
O'Hagan, Andrew 35
On the Origin of Species 19
Ouija boards 49

Page-Lieberman, J. 110
Parkland (2018) 58
Parsons, Charlie 35
Peterson, Scot 60
Phoenix House 13
Piaget, Jean 49
Pilling, T. 108
Pius XII, Pope 92
Plutarch 17
Poulton, R. 50
Prigerson, H. 81, 99, 104, 112–113
Prins, Hans 25
prolonged grief 21
PTSD 58–59, 74, 102, 104
Putin, Vladimir 56

Rådestad, I. 109
Radloff, L. 91
Ramos, Salvador 61, 62, 63, 64
Rando, T. 89

Printed in the United States
by Baker & Taylor Publisher Services